HEAR GOD'S VOICE

Colette Toach

AMI BOOKSHOP

www.ami-bookshop.com

8 Ways to Hear God's Voice

Author: Colette Toach
Graphics & Cover Design: Jessica Toach

ISBN-13: 978-1-62664-238-6

Other formats of this book:
eBook ISBN: 978-1-62664-239-3
Kindle ISBN: 978-1-62664-240-9
iBook ISBN: 978-1-62664-241-6

Copyright © 2021 by Apostolic Movement International, LLC
All rights reserved
5663 Balboa Ave #416,
San Diego,
California 92111,
United States of America

1st Printing March 2021

Published by **Apostolic Movement International, LLC**
E-mail Address: admin@ami-bookshop.com
Web Address: www.ami-bookshop.com

Unless otherwise specified, all Scripture references are taken from the New King James Version®. Copyright © 1982 by Thomas Nelson. Used by permission. All rights reserved.

CONTENTS

1

YOUR CHRISTIAN FOUNDATION

We had a very interesting experience a couple of years back. My father kept having a problem with his house's front door. It would get stuck every time he closed it. So, my husband, Craig, who was also our handyman, came to the rescue with his bag of tools and a wood plane. He started by taking the door off its hinges.

Next, he sanded and planed it, to then fit the door back in correctly. It was a perfect fit. It worked beautifully... for the first two minutes!

After we had opened and closed the door a few times, it got stuck again. So once again, he took the door off its hinges, sanded and planed it, fitted and measured it.

He is very analytical. So, trust me when I say, he did a very good job and took a very long time. Each time, the door was fine for the first few swings, but then it got stuck again. My husband sat there thinking, "What am I doing wrong?"

I was standing on the inside of the house and he was on the outside. Suddenly, I noticed a huge crack in the wall next to the door frame. In fact, the crack was so big I could see right through the wall to the outside where Craig was standing.

I peeked around and said, "Craig, I think we just found our problem."

You see, the wall had started to split and was pushing against the door post. The foundation of the house had started to sink, and so the walls had started to pull apart. Needless to say, my parents moved shortly after.

Building a Strong House

Many Christians have a house that looks like the one I described. It has cracks and lacks a solid foundation. You are trying to learn how to bring it all together. I want to help you do that with the teachings contained in this book.

I don't just want to show you how to build a solid foundation, but also how to build a solid house.

How do you build this house, so that you do not have cracks in your walls? How do you build this house correctly, so that you are doing what God wants you to do?

I will teach you how to hear God clearly, in eight different ways. By the time you have applied these simple principles, you will never ask yourself again, "What is God's will for my life? What has God called me to do?"

You will know what God's will is for your life. From hearing Him through the Urim and Thummim to seeing His plan for you in the Word, you will realize that the Lord has been speaking to you all along. All you need to do now is to learn how to listen.

You Are Invited to the Treasure House

Matthew 13:44 Again, the kingdom of heaven is like treasure hidden in a field, which a man found and hid; and for joy over it he goes and sells all that he has and buys that field.

When you hunger to hear God's voice, what you are really saying is, "Jesus I want to know you." There is no greater revival-starting, life-changing prayer to begin with!

It is only when you hear His voice for yourself that you come to understand the Father, God, and Savior He is! Perhaps you don't realize this, but the Lord will speak to you in a way that you can understand. In other words, the relationship you have with the Lord Jesus won't look anything like the relationship your brother or sister has with Him.

Jesus stretches out His hand to you from this page onward to encounter Him and discover the treasure He has hidden just for you. Not only has He called you from you mother's womb, but He has shaped you by His hand and delights to speak to you in a way that you understand.

So, dump the idea that you have to try really hard to hear Him. Nothing could be further from the truth.

PILLAR POINT:

Jesus is doing all the heavy lifting! He desires to speak to you even more than you want to hear Him!

He won't speak to you because of your righteousness. He won't speak to you because of your calling or anointing. He won't speak to you because of who your parents are.

Jesus delights to speak to you because of who He is. He delights to fellowship with you because you are His creation. So, the first step? Come to peace and enter into this new adventure with the firm conviction that not only does the Lord want to talk to you today, but that He has been waiting for a very long time to tell you the secrets He has been holding onto, just for you!

2

#1 HEARING GOD THROUGH THE WORD

I f you want to build a solid wall you need cement. Have you ever been to a building site? There are big bags of cement piled up all over the place. Cement is hard and strong. Just as cement establishes a firm foundation in the natural, in the same way, the Word of God is that cement in our lives too!

So, it stands to reason that hearing God through the Word adds a solid foundation to your life.

Growing up I constantly heard people teach that the Word is God's voice speaking to me. At church they said, "You need to read the Word. The Bible is the voice of God. If you read the Bible, you will know what to do in your daily life."

So, you read the Bible and think, "Who cares about Noah? Who cares about Gideon? Right now, I have marital problems. Right now, I need to know if I need to move across the country."

Sometimes you feel like you are reading a bunch of stories. While the Word lays a solid doctrinal foundation with good Christian principles to live by, is it possible to hear God through it for solutions to today's problems?

I know for myself, that Apostle Paul felt so ahead of me spiritually. I felt for the longest time that he could never understand what I was going through. Sure, he taught good principles for our spiritual lives, but when rent is overdue or your child is in the hospital, you need to hear Jesus... now!

When the Lord began to reveal Himself to me through the Word, I came to a revelation that "the word of God is living and powerful, and sharper than any two-edged sword, piercing even to the division of soul and spirit, and of joints and marrow, and is a discerner of the thoughts and intents of the heart" (Heb. 4:12).

Scripture is not a string of well positioned words on a page. It contains the very nature of the Lord Jesus Christ and when you hear Him through the Word, you develop a relationship with Him that adds security to your life.

PILLAR POINT:

You don't need to be a teacher to hear God's voice through the Word! If you have Jesus dwelling within you, then all sixty-six books are talking to you about your problems today!

The million dollar question is though... how? If you know me well enough, you know that this is my happy place! Let me not get sidetracked on how excited I am about the Word, but move on to teaching you how to take hold of its secrets for your life today!

Understanding the Language of the Word

The first thing you need to do when you are reading the Word is to feed pictures into your mind. You keep looking at the Word of God as just words. Since the beginning of time, God has been speaking in types and shadows.

Even when Jesus walked the earth, what did He use to communicate with us? Parables. Why do you think that is? It is because we understand pictures.

I bet you can remember the last movie you watched more than the last sermon you heard. In my introduction, I shared the story of the house with the crack in the wall. You will remember those pictures.

As you go along in your journey, that picture will come to your mind and you will ask, "Lord, what are you telling me?" He will use that picture to talk to you.

If you want to understand the language of the Word, do not think it is about what version of the Bible you read. You have to understand that it is a language of pictures. You need to learn to visualize the Word.

When you read the Scriptures, visualize what is happening. Picture yourself in that situation. Travel back in time with me here.

Apostle Paul is preaching a long sermon late into the night. Can you see yourself huddled in the upper room? It's way past your bedtime and everyone is yawning. You look across the room and see a young guy sitting on the windowsill. You think to yourself, "Hmm, that looks a bit dangerous."

As Paul drones on, good old Eutychus falls asleep and falls out that window. You hear a terrible *thud* as he hits the ground and the shocking reality strikes that he just fell out the window and killed himself.

Today's breaking news would read, "Young man is preached to death by traveling apostle."

Just when you thought you had a bad day at church...

Immerse Yourself Into the World of the Word

Can you imagine the panic? See yourself surging ahead of the frantic crowd as you rush outside to where Eutychus is lying.

You arrive and watch as Paul embraces him and raises the dead boy up. Then? Paul returns to breaking bread and keeps preaching until daybreak! (I'm guessing Eutychus found a different seat for the remainder of the meeting.)

I bet you will never forget that Scripture (Acts 20:7-12).

You see, it is not enough to just picture the Word, but you have to immerse yourself in it.

PILLAR POINT:

When you position yourself as an active participant of the Scriptures, it becomes part of your story.

Something happens when you put yourself in the Word. You feel the emotion of it. What you are doing is engaging your entire soul. You are bringing your soul into subjection to the Word.

When you do this, you are not simply reading or understanding the Word. Rather, you are feeling the Word.

When you do that, the Word comes alive to you. Jesus is manifested in the Word. The Word is alive. You can feel it. You can experience, taste, and smell it.

Can you see Peter walking to the temple after the day of Pentecost? Can you hear the hustle and bustle of the marketplace? Can you smell the scent of someone's cooking as Peter walks by on his way?

It is dirty and dusty. There is a crippled guy on the side of the road. He has not bathed in months and is begging for any scraps he can find. Peter stops and says, "Silver and gold I do not have, but what I do have I give you" (Acts 3:6).

You are there. Can you see the man leap and walk? Maybe he does not have all his teeth, sporting a big, gummy smile. Can you imagine the cripple's excitement as he leaps and praises God?

What a commotion! Next thing you know, everyone who is within eyeshot of what happened gets caught up in the excitement and joins in, dancing all the way to the temple!

Wow, I am so excited visualizing this. I want to go raise somebody up right now!

See? God is speaking to you through the Word. It is not good enough to say, "I read my chapter of the Word today." No, you must immerse yourself in it.

I am one of those crazy types who loves the books of Numbers and Leviticus. I can picture them.

When I read them, I can see this poor guy coming to the priests with a problem and the priests advise, "You must go home, shave, wash, and quarantine for seven days!" (A tad ahead of their time, eh?)

It gives me a picture of what it must have been like to live in that day and age under those laws. Imagine having to live by those guidelines and rules. Visualizing myself in Numbers and Leviticus immerses me in the culture of their time. Once I am in their time, I perceive the Scriptures through eyes that are generations past.

However, if you are just reading the Word with your own understanding, you won't hone in on what Jesus is telling you intimately, because the Lord speaks in pictures that make sense to you. So, every time you read the Scriptures, immerse yourself.

We live in a modern age and videos are everywhere. So, make a video in your mind. Say to yourself, "If I had to make a movie of this chapter, how would I depict it? Which actor would I cast for the main part? What character would I play?"

Suddenly, the Word is not a law that brings death. Rather, it is living, powerful, and sharper than any two-edged sword.

However, it won't become powerful or living until you make it so. Let me tell you, the devil knows the Bible better than you! So, you would think he would be born again by now, wouldn't you? Just reading the Word is not enough.

> ## PILLAR POINT:
>
> There are many people who have read the Word, but do not know the power of it because they do not feed it into their spirit.

How do you feed something into your spirit? The same way you get something out of your spirit. Through your five senses.

Engage All Five Senses

Feed the Word into your spirit using all five senses. How cold was Paul drifting in the ocean for a full day and night? During the day, did the sun beat down on his bare head (2 Cor. 11:25)?

Feed the Word into your spirit through what you see, taste, smell, touch, and hear. That is how we deposit the things of God into our spirit and rewrite our reality.

You know what is exciting about this practice? You will be doing life, when suddenly the Lord will press rewind and play.

Suddenly, the movie you pushed into your spirit a year ago will pop up into your mind.

Guess what? The Lord just spoke to you through His Word. You are waiting for the "thus saith the Lord" message.

Many have the idea that hearing God through the Word means that they will wake up to the Lord saying, "Go to Psalms chapter 2 verse 3."

Then they will have to quickly look through the Word. "What is God telling me?"

It certainly happens, but it's only when you have learned the language of the Word that it will have the power to renew your mind and speak into your life today.

There is a reason the Word is so pictorial. It's packed full of stories and illustrations – some are rather graphic!

Read the Song of Solomon. There is nothing left hidden to the imagination in that book! The language of it though... Studying the Song of Solomon gives you insight into the language of the Spirit.

Solomon did not simply say, "I love you," to his bride.

He said, "Your hair is as lovely as a flock of goats."

(This apparently was a compliment in that age. In our modern era... not so much.)

The point is, he painted pictures that express the Lord's language.

The Word Will Come Out as Rhema

Faith comes by hearing, and hearing, by the rhema word of God. First, you have to put those words into your spirit, and then, once those pictures come back out, faith is formed because they will come out as rhema.

It may go in as logos or even just as your imagination. You may not even feel any anointing on it at first. However, when that word comes out, it will come out as rhema. It will come out in power, in the right place, and at the right time.

Have you ever experienced this in your walk with God before? You listened to a message or read a book but didn't really get anything out of it at the time.

Then somewhere along the road, something happens, and you say, "You know, this situation reminds me of a story I read. It reminds me of something that preacher shared with me."

The Lord just spoke to you. This is a powerful way to hear the Lord's voice, and you are neglecting it. Now, let me get to the next point, otherwise I will carry on with this because it is my favorite way to hear God's voice. I am sure you can tell...

Make the Word fun! Make it alive in you and let God speak to you!

RAPID RECAP

1. *When you read the Word, visualize yourself in the time it was written.*

2. *What do you imagine it smells like?*

3. *What sounds surround you?*

4. *Is there a familiar taste (honey, milk, etc.) associated with this passage?*

5. *Is it cold or hot? What do you feel?*

6. *Most importantly, what do you see? If you made a movie of this passage, what would the set look like?*

READING THE WORD
WITH INTENT

Y ou are immersed in the Word and without realizing it, you have come face to face with the Lord in a way that rewrites your mind! In fact, you just touched a part of His heart that not many experience.

Knowing our heavenly Father's law brings us closer to Him and as you sort through all that input, the question remains, "How do I get a direct answer through the Word for my problem today?"

This is the key you are looking for.

PILLAR POINT:

Don't just read the Word at random. Read it with intent.

This means reading the Word deliberately for a specific reason. Say for example that you have a financial need. Perhaps you are battling with bitterness, lust, or you have a conflict with your spouse.

Pick up the Word with that question in your mind. Read the Word and expect to find the answer there. Now, you might not always find the answer in the first Scripture or two.

I approach the Word like this: I exercise my faith and say, "Lord, I need a direct answer for this crisis. Lord, I need something more than a vision. I need something solid that I can stand on and confess."

Then, I pick up the Word and begin reading. I will leaf through several books of the Bible.

I will go from chapter to chapter and let my eyes skim the pages until the right verse hits me at the right time. It will be the exact answer to my problem.

Read in Faith

Now, the key to that one is to read in faith and to keep your question in mind. Many people have the impression that if God wanted to say something to them, He would just jump out and say it.

So, they read the Word thinking, "Okay God, say something to me!" Well, that is not a very nice conversation. When I have a good conversation with someone, it is a permission-based conversation.

I ask you something and then you ask me something. I do not just walk up to someone and tell them what I want them to do without saying hello first. Unless, of course, I have not had my morning cup of coffee and I am in the mood to boss someone around... needless to say, it doesn't usually work out well for me!

The Lord won't do that to you. He won't impose His Word on you. He doesn't suddenly jump on you, or shout at you. He is not that kind of God. He is a loving, tender God.

He wants to converse with you. So, when you come to Him with a question, He will give you the answer. When you read the Word this way, it can take a bit of time.

The more you get used to flowing this way, the quicker you will find the right Scripture at the right time. When you find it, that Scripture will become an anchor point in your life.

Discovering Keynote Scriptures for Life

I remember one time when I was battling with a huge attack on my mind. My dreams were full of nightmares and while I was going through the day, terrible thoughts would come at me.

My mind was a complete battlefield. I took authority, I prayed, and I struggled. I said, "Lord, you have to help me." I started reading through the Word and I came to the Scripture about casting down imaginations and every high thing that exalts itself above the glory of God and bringing every thought into captivity to the obedience of Christ (2 Cor. 10:5).

Wow! That set me on fire. I exclaimed, "That is it! That is my answer!" Then I prayed, "Satan, you lose your hold because I bring into captivity, every thought that's not in line with Christ!"

I am very pictorial, so I saw thoughts assailing me from every side. I grabbed them, put them in prison and brought them into captivity under Christ, and God had the key. Just like that, I was free.

Every time I had one of those thoughts again, that Scripture came to mind and I brought those thoughts into captivity like snatching birds from the air and putting them in a cage. After that, I stopped having attacks on my mind.

21

It took the Word to give me that kind of power. I needed that anchor. When you read the Word of God with intent, you will get the kind of Scriptures that will become keynotes in your life. They will become pillars in your life that keep you anchored.

Guess what? You just heard from God. You keep thinking that hearing from God in this way is this super-duper experience that only high-level apostles can have. If that were the case, then why did the Lord take the time to put the Scriptures together in the first place?

You have already been hearing from the Lord. You just need to identify it. With a little practice, you will be fluent in the language of the Word.

Forming New Templates Through Memorization

The final way to hear the Lord through the Scriptures is to form new templates. You need to form new molds in your mind for success and blessing. There is no easy way around this. It takes a little work. It takes some memorization of Scripture.

It is a lot like reading the Word and making a movie out of it like I shared earlier. You need to do that deliberately with specific Scriptures. The Scripture you use will depend on what you are struggling with.

Maybe you want to understand doctrine or are trying to figure out your calling. Maybe, you are battling with sin in your life or struggling with finances.

Step 1: Read With Intent

Begin by reading the Word with intent. As you do this, Scriptures are going to pop up and when they do, write them down.

Step 2: Memorize Scriptures That Pop Up

Then, after you write the Scriptures down, start to memorize them.

Step 3: Visualize the Scripture as You Memorize It

As you memorize that Scripture, make a movie of it in your mind and see yourself in it, and continually speak it out. Continue to push it into your spirit.

Perhaps the Scripture you are memorizing is Mark 11:23:

> *For assuredly, I say to you, whoever says to this mountain, 'Be removed and be cast into the sea,' and does not doubt in his heart, but believes that those things he says will be done, he will have whatever he says.*

Each time you quote it, envision that mountain being thrown into the sea!

The next time you are in prayer you say, "Lord, what did I do? Where did I go wrong? What happened?" Suddenly, the picture of the mountain that you were pushing into your spirit will come to your mind.

What is the Lord saying? The verse said that, "Whoever says to this mountain be removed..."

He is saying, "Remove the mountain!" You just heard the voice of God through the Word!

Do you see why pictures are so important?

PILLAR POINT:

If you are not using the Word as your cement, you will find a nice big crack in your wall, because if the pictures are not based on the Word, then what are they based on?

What Are You Basing Your Pictures On?

Think about all the pictures you fed into your spirit within the last forty-eight hours. I guarantee the pictures came from books you read, conversations you had, or movies you watched.

What are you giving God to work with? What cement does He have to build your house with? If you do not learn to hear God through the Word first, then learning to hear God in the next two ways won't make any sense to you.

Cement comes first. The Word is our basis and our foundation. Once you can hear God through the Word, the next step, which is hearing God through the Spirit, becomes so much easier.

RAPID RECAP

1. *Read in faith, expecting an answer.*
2. *Read with a clear question in your mind (read with intent).*
3. *Make a note of and memorize the Scriptures that leap out at you.*
4. *As you quote the Scriptures, visualize them down to the smallest detail.*

#2 HEARING GOD THROUGH THE URIM AND THUMMIM

I n this day and age everyone is quite amazed by the gifts of the Spirit. I am not knocking the gifts, I love them. In fact, we have a couple of schools where we teach on them. However, if you do not go to the Word first, you won't have a solid foundation from which to build.

Do you know why? It is because the Spirit is like water. When you get cement in those big bags, you have to mix it with water. Then the cement sets. You need the two together.

I see such an imbalance in the church. I see people with countless bags of cement, thinking that cement alone will build them a house. Then on the opposite extreme, I see believers with countless jugs of water who think that water alone will build them a house.

The Spirit of God Activates the Word

You need the Spirit of God to activate the knowledge of the Word. Only then, will you discover wisdom in its purity. However, if you do not have enough Word in you, what is the Spirit going to activate? Nothing!

You will just get into deception because you will base all of your decisions on feelings, impressions, impulses and good ideas, instead of on the Scriptures you have fed into your spirit.

Also, when that picture comes out, is it a picture that you fed in using the Scriptures? Or, is the picture that comes out based on something you got from the world, which the enemy can easily manipulate?

Find the Balance

You have two imbalances. The first imbalanced view says, "All you need is the Word, the Word, the Word!"

I don't know about you, but I have never seen anyone build a house with cement bags. It would not be a secure house, because without water, cement can be blown away like dust.

However, if you take some water and mix that in, a reaction takes place. The cement sets and becomes so solid and hard, that it won't crack.

If you are imbalanced on either side, then you are like the house that had a big crack in the wall. Why? It is because the cement could not take the pressure. It was not mixed right. Something went wrong. The balance was all wrong.

We have a lot of teaching already on hearing God through the spirit. It is great to hear Him that way, but if you are just going on the spirit alone and have no Word in you, what is being activated?

You may have a rock on which to build the house, which is Jesus Christ. However, you have no house. We are the temples of the Holy Ghost. If we want to be a solid house on the rock, we need to build with the proper amount of cement and water.

PILLAR POINT:

Revelation always confirms the Word. Do not think you can do it with the Word alone, because water brings life. Water activates.

Using Principles Effectively

So many people ask me, after they have gone through the teachings, "How do I know the correct time to apply specific principles? It seems that there is so much that I have to keep in my head."

It's good that you have all that knowledge, but it takes wisdom to make that knowledge work. The Spirit of God is the only one who can cause that kind of reaction in your life.

If you are not getting any wisdom, then you are too dry. All you have is principles, principles, and more principles! On the other hand, if you do not have anything solid and you keep being swayed by your emotions, then you are just water, water, and more water.

God Wants to Converse With You!

It is not so complicated. Hearing His voice is the inheritance of every child of God. What is the first thing that parents do when a baby is born? They embrace their baby and make the most ridiculous noises you have ever heard.

29

They talk to the child right away. They talk to the baby while it is still in the belly. If we as natural parents cuddle and speak to our babies to let them know that we are there, then how much more our heavenly Father?

You think you have to earn the right to hear His voice or somehow be spiritual and righteous enough before He will tell you His great will. No, He is making those *baby* sounds to you all the time. You are just not listening.

He is a loving and tender father. He is speaking. He is giving you impressions. He is letting pictures from the Word pop up in your mind all the time. You might wonder, "What am I thinking about that for?"

Hello...? The Lord was talking to you! It is so simple. Then after you learn to listen to the impressions in your spirit, the next things to flow in, are visions and journaling. These two go hand in hand. First though let us dig into the easiest way to hear His voice: through your spiritual Urim and Thummim.

God Doesn't Play Favorites

There is nothing more damaging in a family than when parents play favorites. I have personally worked with a lot of people who had this experience growing up and it can really mess you up.

It messes with your perception of life, relationships, and even your view of marriage.

Unfortunately, it is a sad truth that there are many believers who had parents who played favorites. When you are not the favorite, you grow up with the idea that there are some people in this world who are special and who have things handed to them and then... there are the rest of us.

We are the ones who have to work hard to get what we want in life.

The problem with this kind of upbringing is that you view God in this way too. You start to think that God has favorites.

When it comes to hearing God's voice, you can work yourself into a frenzy. You find yourself trying so hard to hear from Him, to get some of His attention that you miss one important fact.

Your heavenly Father is not like your natural father.

You don't have to be a little child pulling at his pant leg desperately trying to get His attention, shouting, "Daddy, look at me!"

Your heavenly Father is not like that. In fact, He is the kind of parent, who when you are ignoring and rejecting Him, and running your own way, runs after you to get your attention.

When you least expect it, you turn to find Him reaching down to pick you up and to give you love you did not deserve.

God Wants to Speak to You

However, you have this image of the Lord that is based on your relationship with your natural father. It's based on your upbringing, and on how you have been programmed to view the world. This thinking says, "God gives revelation to some and not others. The heavenly Father speaks to some and not others."

I want to smash this wrong concept. Our Father does not speak to some and not to others. He is not a father who will have a conversation with one child and not speak to the other.

He wants to speak to you. He wants to communicate with you. This is the first conviction that you need to get, when coming to hear God's voice.

Not only does He want to speak to you, but He is already speaking to you all the time!

PILLAR POINT:

You don't need to keep trying so hard. The truth is that it is your very trying and striving that is blocking God's voice in your life.

You are not hearing Him because you are so busy running around trying to get His attention that you neither hear nor see the obvious that is right in front of you.

There is a big thrust in the church concerning prophetic revelation. There is a lot of emphasis on the gifts and on getting revelation for others.

That's fantastic and the body of Christ needs it, but until you can come to a place where you can hear His voice for yourself, what do you have to give to others?

Only Hearing for Others Is Not Good Enough

Perhaps you have learned to minister to others and to get revelation on their behalf. Unfortunately, when it comes to your personal life, it feels like you always fall short of the mark.

You feel that you are not spiritual or holy enough for God to speak to you about your own life.

Here is a vital fact to remember: The day you were born again, you became as holy and righteous as Jesus Christ because you stand in His blood.

When you stand in Christ and the Father looks at you, do you know what He sees? He sees the blood of Christ and that cleanses you from all sin, all unrighteousness, and you stand as perfect before His eyes just as Jesus Christ Himself is sinless and pure. (Go read 1 John 1 for a confirmation on that.)

He looks upon you with love, and He wants to speak to you. If you can get that conviction, then you are well on your way to hearing God's voice for yourself.

If you can stop the striving for a moment, you might even realize that He has been talking to you all along.

You have been so busy running around, while all along the Lord has been standing right by your side saying, "Hello... I have been standing here for some time. If you would just be quiet and come and listen, you would hear my voice."

Expect the Unexpected

Perhaps the way you are hearing God's voice is not how you expected to hear Him. That is what this particular book is about. Especially the first few chapters are all about teaching you how to identify the Lord's voice in your life.

I won't move on to the topic of sharing with others until you have learned to master this in your own life.

By the end of this chapter, you will jump up and down saying, "I have been hearing His voice!"

Once you get that conviction, your spiritual life will take off in a hundred directions. God hasn't been silent. God hasn't been ignoring you. God doesn't have favorites.

The Urim and Thummim

> **1 Samuel 28:6** *And when Saul inquired of the Lord, the Lord did not answer him, either by dreams or by Urim or by the prophets.*

> **Exodus 28:30** *And you shall put in the breastplate of judgment the Urim and the Thummim, and they shall be over Aaron's heart when he goes in before the Lord [...]*

In the Old Testament, the Lord instructed Moses to make a special robe for Aaron to perform his priestly duties in. The breastplate was by far its most fascinating part. You can read all the details in Exodus 28, but I want to draw your attention to the Urim and Thummim that are mentioned.

Tradition suggests that they were two smooth stones, one black, the other white. Depending on which one Aaron pulled out, would give you God's direct answer.

You will see this mentioned a number of times in the Old Testament. It was a wonderful way for the children of Israel to get a direct answer from the Lord. When they needed a *yes* or *no* answer about something, they would pay Aaron a visit. He would then slip his hand into his breastplate and pull out either the Urim or the Thummim.

Getting an Urim from the Lord meant *yes* and a Thummim *no*. Wouldn't it be nice to have a set of these stones hanging around in your sock drawer for emergencies? Well, the good news is that we have something way better than that.

From the time the Holy Spirit came to dwell inside of you, He brought along His Urim and Thummim and deposited them directly into your spirit. Aaron wore the stones over his heart - a symbol of what we now have through Christ - an inheritance inside our hearts!

> **Ephesians 6:14-15** *Stand therefore, having girded your waist with truth, having put on the breastplate of righteousness, and having shod your feet with the preparation of the gospel of peace.*

Today, every believer gets to wear the breastplate! With the indwelling of the Holy Spirit comes the ability to get a straight answer from the Lord.

Relating It to the Urim and Thummim

This is how the Urim and Thummim work. God is simply speaking through your spirit and influencing the emotions in your soul. (For more detail on this please read the *Prophetic Functions*[1] book.)

The Lord specifically speaks through the *emotion function* of your soul when He gives you an Urim or Thummim. When He speaks to you in this way, you will experience a deep gut feeling of *yes* or one of *no*.

Just think back on some life-changing experiences. I guarantee that during these times you either had a deep sense of peace or a deep sense of foreboding. Well, that was your Urim or Thummim talking.

The Lord was giving you the *yes/no* answer you were looking for. In fact, once you make it a practice to listen to the influence of your spirit, you will realize that you get these deep feelings throughout your day.

Listening to Your Spirit

The key with the Urim and Thummim is to be sensitive to the spirit. I think that we tend to run ahead of the Lord.

Our mind gets in the way, and we get an idea of what we should be doing. Before the Lord has a chance to speak to us, we are off... changing the world. It is only when we hit that big, fat wall that we realize, "Actually, I should have listened to my spirit."

This is something that you should be developing on a daily basis. What is fantastic about the spiritual Urim and Thummim is that you can use this twenty-four hours a day. The Holy Spirit is speaking to you constantly. He is telling you what direction to take in every part of your life.

Don't only use the Urim and Thummim when you are ministering, or when you specifically need direction. I want you to be aware of the Urim and Thummim in your spirit all the time and for every decision you make.

Let's look at some practical places where you will use the Urim and Thummim.

Intercession

You get prayer warriors who spend more time making prayer lists than they do praying. They make their list so long that just reading through it casually takes an hour.

They rush into prayer, with every intent of storming the gates of heaven and breaking down the gates of hell.

I can imagine the Lord standing there thinking, "Wow, that looks quite intense. I wonder if they will allow me to get a word in there…?" Half the time the burdens you are praying for are not even of the Lord.

He should not need to shout from the heavens, "You are praying in the wrong direction!" If you just stopped for a minute to hear what your spirit is saying, you would know if you are praying right or not.

So, before you attack every demon in hell and bring every person on your list before God, ask yourself, "Do I feel an Urim or do I feel a Thummim on this?"

Try this the next time you pray. When you come to intercede for someone who asked you to pray for them, ask yourself, "What do I sense in my spirit?"

Do you feel, "Yeah, yeah! Now is the time to pray," or do you feel, "Hmm… the time is not yet"?

If you feel an Urim in intercession, the words will tumble out of your mouth effortlessly. If it is a Thummim, you will feel like it is stopped up with cotton wool!

Why would the Lord give you a Thummim? Perhaps the circumstances are not right; perhaps your faith is not strong enough; perhaps that person's faith is not at full capacity yet.

Learn to listen to your spirit. Learn to discern when you are going in either the right or the wrong direction.

Experiencing the Thummim

You know, so often I have come to the Lord in prayer, even with emergencies. "Lord, we have this financial crisis, and we have this health crisis." You come to pray, and you feel as if there is cotton wool in your mouth. You just can't seem to find your words.

You feel like you are hitting a wall in the spirit. When this happens, the Lord is saying, "Not now."

"But Lord, this is an emergency!"

"Not now. Now is not the time."

If you push through and ignore the warning bells, you will just speak empty words. I promise you will feel exhausted in the end.

Experiencing the Urim

Then there will be times when a thought will pop up in your mind while you are praying. You might see a vision of someone you know. Then, you casually hold them up praying, "Lord, I just want to bless my sister..."

Bam! You feel a waterfall flowing out of your belly. You know that you are praying in the right direction. In fact, you feel charged with electricity.

Revelation flows, decrees come forth, and the anointing comes down.

Wouldn't it be exciting if every time you prayed, you prayed with power, and experienced that excitement? Well, if you are praying in God's will and in His direction, you will always feel that power.

Prayer should revive and invigorate you. If you keep coming away exhausted, you are not listening to your Urim and Thummim.

Daily Life

God wants to be involved in every part of your life. He wants to be involved in your daily decision-making, which is where you can also use the Urim and Thummim.

"Lord, should I pay this bill or that one?"

"Lord, should I move to this town or that one?"

Does this seem trivial? Absolutely! However, when you are with your spouse or a friend, is it trivial to ask them, "What do you think, we should do? Should we go here or there?"

So, if you can ask your spouse or a friend, then why not the Lord? Is He not your bridegroom? Is He not your friend?

If you just integrate the Lord into every area of your life and take His voice seriously, you will experience Him in a whole new way.

You will see the Lord move in your life. You will no longer just know of Him or just understand the principles, but you will come to know Him in an intimate way.

Make the Lord part of your decision-making, wherever you go this week and whatever decision you make.

Okay... also have some balance! This is not license for you to get paranoid. Don't be afraid to take a step because you didn't hear a Urim or Thummim!

I am not saying that you should go to an extreme, I am saying that you should become sensitive to what you hear in your spirit.

Start involving the Lord in every part of your life and listen to your spirit! Listen before you run off in one of your hundred directions. There is not always time to sit down and receive an elaborate answer from the Lord.

The Urim and Thummim will remain with you regardless of how many other ways you learn to hear the Lord through.

RAPID RECAP

1. *The Word is activated by the Spirit.*
2. *The Urim and Thummim are part of the breast-plate of righteousness.*
3. *Listen to your spirit for the yes or no answers from God.*
4. *The Urim and Thummim give you the next step to take. The revelation is progressive.*

#3 HEARING GOD THROUGH DREAMS

Job 33:15 In a dream, in a vision of the night, when deep sleep falls upon men, while slumbering on their beds.

Dreams are common to many believers and also the next easiest way to hear God's voice (if you know how to interpret them of course).

Once you have mastered dream interpretation, you should then move on from there and develop hearing from God in every other way.

Moving Into Dreams

Let's hear from the Lord in every way possible and if you don't flow in dreams yet, desire it.

In fact, many who are reading this, do not realize God speaks to us in our dreams! So, allow me to uncover this secret and then move you on to even deeper revelations.

Understanding Dreams

With that being said, I will give you the gist of the main points of dream interpretation. If you have already read my book *The Way of Dreams and Visions*[2] you can skip this part and move straight to the next chapter.

If not, dig in and allow the Holy Spirit to put some things into perspective for you.

The biggest mistake most people make when trying to interpret dreams is to assume that everything and everyone they dream about represents that very thing/person.

PILLAR POINT:

The most important principle to remember is that most of your dreams fall into a category called, internal dreams. This means that every person, place, and object in that dream are a representation of a part of your life.

So, if you dream that your sister-in-law has a baby, please do not bash down her door to tell her the good news! Your dreams are a picture of your life. Your sister-in-law represents a part of yourself, as does that baby.

Understanding the Parables

The Word is full of types and shadows. The Lord Jesus Himself spoke in parables.

Your dreams are also like parables. The Lord is telling you a story to get His message across to you. In the same way that Jesus' parables had deeper meanings, so do your dreams.

When Jesus shared the parable of the Good Samaritan, it would have been odd for someone in the crowd to rush out and try to find the real man Jesus was talking about.

No, the parable was clear. Jesus was telling a story, using pictures they could relate to, so He could get a message across to them. The same holds true for your dreams. The Lord is using pictures that are common to you and to the Word to give you a message.

The first step to understand your dreams is to categorize them.

4 Steps to Dream Interpretation

Step 1: Categorizing Your Dreams

Before you can understand what the characters in your dream represent, it is a good idea to categorize the dream first. You need to identify if it a prophetic, a healing, a garbage/purging, or internal dream.

Let's look at some hints on how to identify which category a dream falls into.

A. Prophetic

A prophetic dream is very clear. It is a short, clear dream with a single message. You might have a few short dreams one after the other, each containing a similar message.

The most outstanding aspect of a prophetic dream is that you are not a participant. In dreams like this, you will find yourself standing on the outside watching the events.

This kind of dream concerns future events. It functions like the word of wisdom and needs to be applied discerningly. The dreams Daniel had are prime examples for this category. He received external prophetic dreams with regards to Israel and the empires of his time. His dreams always had a future orientation.

Joseph also interpreted the King of Egypt's external dream, which allowed him to save many lives, even the lives of his nation. Note how even external dreams were given in symbolism! Even in an external dream the characters may not be who they are in real life.

B. Healing

In a healing dream you will most likely relive past events. Perhaps you will go back to past houses, or time frames in your life, and relive an event, but this time with a happy ending.

If you dream that you are running or hiding, but then finally confront that which is chasing you, you are having a healing dream.

You might even wake up crying or laughing after a dream like this.

C. Garbage and Purging Dreams

If you have a dream that is overcomplicated with many changes of scenery and events, your inner man is very likely *throwing out* the junk it accumulated that day.

You will likely have many garbage dreams when you get into the Word more and spend more time with the Lord. Your mind will make space for the Word but will *throw out* the garbage you had stored in there for years.

If you dream that you are displaying emotions and character-istics that are not natural to you, your subconscious is simply *living out* feelings and hidden temptations you experienced during the day. These dreams are called purging dreams and do not have an interpretation.

D. Internal Dreams

The most outstanding characteristic of an internal dream is that you are the *star of the show*.

Apart from garbage dreams, this dream type is the most common.

Sometimes they are simply a picture of what is going on in your spirit at the time. However, prophets often receive di-rection for the future in these kinds of dreams.

So, in identifying if your dream falls under the internal dreams category, ask yourself, "Was I the main star?"

If that is the case, the dream is internal, and the characters are symbolic of something in your life.

An internal dream will often give you direction for your spir-itual life. It functions the same way as a word of knowledge. It relates things of the past and present to you.

It will let you know if you got off the path, or if you need to place more emphasis on something. It will give you an idea of what state your spirit is in and if there is something lacking in your life.

It may also tell you when you have birthed something new, or have come to a place of rest, or promotion.

The Internal Prophetic Dream

An internal prophetic dream has a slightly different emphasis. Joseph's dreams of his brothers' sheaves bowing to his, are a good example of this. The Lord gave him these dreams to indicate that his family would one day bow before him.

These dreams were internal because they concerned him personally, but they were also prophetic because they were giving him a word for the future.

Another good example would be the baker and butler's dreams. Joseph interpreted those dreams in prison (Gen. 40:5). Both dreams concerned them personally, but also gave prophetic words of what was going to happen.

An internal prophetic dream functions the same way as a word of wisdom, only that the word pertains to you personally. The symbols in your dream represent a part of yourself.

STEP 2: Sensing the Spirit

Next, sense the spirit on the dream. Was there a negative or a positive spirit? Was there a sense of peace, joy, fear, death, life, change, or insecurity? This step is more relevant than you realize.

This point is applicable to both dreams and visions. The spirit of the dream can change the interpretation completely.

Consider the vision Peter had of the blanket being lowered with all the unclean animals (Acts 10:14).

You would expect the connotation of this vision to be negative, but instead, it was positive. Eating the unclean animals was portrayed as a good thing. The Lord was trying to tell

Peter that what He considered unclean (the Gentiles) God had cleansed by His blood.

What if the vision had been negative? If this vision was a warning, it could well have meant that Peter was tempted to partake in something unclean and that he should avoid it. Can you see how, in the same way, the positive/negative orientation of a dream can change the interpretation entirely?

So, consider your dream. Once you have it categorized, ask yourself, "Did this dream feel good or bad? Did I feel positive or negative?"

STEP 3: Identifying the Symbols

Now you will break the dream down and dissect it. Once you become more accustomed to dream interpretation you won't need to break the dream down as much. You will learn to see the interpretation without having to dig through all the details.

For those who are still learning, it is good to follow these steps, until you learn how to flow by the spirit.

Make yourself a list with the letters A-F. Then under each letter, list the corresponding place, scene, character, object, creature, color, … as they appear in the dream. Reading through the helps I list below, systematically identify the symbol for each point.

Now is a good time to mention that I cover all of the symbols in more detail in my *Dreams and Visions Symbol Dictionary*[3].

A. Places

Make a list of the various places encountered in the dream. You may dream of places that are familiar to you. It could be that the Lord is bringing healing to that part of your life, or that He is exposing something that happened during that time (while you lived there).

Churches can speak of a place of worship. If it is an old style church, it could be speaking of the religious, status quo system. A house could speak of your life, your body as the temple of the Holy Spirit.

Places such as monuments or historical buildings may speak of things relating to the past (things gone by).

You might find yourself running through alleyways or dark streets. This often speaks of running blind and not having direction. If the feeling associated with the place is negative and fearful, it could be that the Lord is revealing to you that the enemy is wreaking havoc in your life and that he is sending you in all sorts of directions... none of which are the Lord's.

If you find yourself in a meadow where the sun is shining and you feel peace, the Lord could be revealing to you that you have entered into a time of rest with Him. This could speak of a time of freedom and escape from the pressure around you.

Each of these would have a specific meaning pertaining to you as an individual. Look to the Lord for revelation concerning what the places you dream about mean to you.

B. Scenes

Write down the scenes of the dream. Once again you might find yourself in a scene that is familiar to you.

While restaurants can speak of being fed, bathrooms can speak of being exposed, or of a season of cleansing in your life. Bedrooms speak of intimacy and privacy. You would need to identify what the scene means to you. Did you sense a positive or negative feeling towards that scene in your dream?

C. Identifying the Characters

Look at each character in the dream and identify what part of you they represent if the dream is internal.

Some Hints:

- If you know the character, then write down your relationship with them or what they mean to you.
- If you don't know the character, note what your impressions were of them in your dream.
- If they are relatives, note how close you are to them. If the character is your spouse, then your relationship with them will determine the symbol. It could be positive or negative. Learn to identify this one because it will recur.

Often your spouse can speak of your recreated spirit in Christ. If you had a really good relationship with your earthly father, he could speak of the Lord in your dreams. If you have a bad relationship with a character, it is possible that they represent your flesh or sinful nature in your dreams.

If you often find yourself dreaming of an unknown man or woman, but yet they seem familiar to you, they could represent your masculine or feminine nature.

The masculine often represents left-brained, intellectual thinking, while the feminine represents the prophetic, right-brained emphasis.

If there is a person in your life who is strong and whom you look up to, they could speak of the Holy Spirit and His protection.

The Relationship Is Vital to Interpretation

Your real-life relationship with the character who shows up in your dream, is vital in identifying what they represent.

Your subconscious will use your emotions and thoughts to convey the appropriate message to you clearly.

Often your subconscious will use people who represent something in your life. Perhaps the music leader in your church could represent your musical gifts. If you are a prophet, you might be at constant loggerheads with your pastor. In that case he could speak of the status quo church system in your dreams.

Often your children speak of your ministry or representations of what you have birthed in the spirit.

Dreaming about giving birth, or being pregnant, can speak of something you are about to birth in the spirit or have given birth to.

If you dream of babies dying it could be a warning dream that something the Lord has given you is dying.

D. Objects

- Note if the object means anything special to you.
- Does the object convey a negative or positive impression to you?

If you keep dreaming of coffins, the Lord might be letting you know that something in your flesh needs to die or has already died but you need to let it go.

This dream is common amongst those in fivefold ministry offices who are called to die to the flesh so that the spirit can dominate.

Dreaming of dead bodies is not always an attack from the enemy but a message from the Lord to let what is corrupt and rotten die!

A wedding ring can speak of a covenant. A wedding dress speaks of your union with the Lord, or things you are *married* or *tied* to.

Furthermore, there are objects from the Word that are often displayed in our dreams. Gold objects speak of the Lord and His deity, while a clay pot speaks of us as His vessels ready for service.

Wine often speaks of the anointing, as do water and oil. Arrows or weapons piercing you can speak of the work of the enemy who is known for his darts of destruction. Wielding a sword speaks of carrying the Lord's authority and using it as a weapon against the enemy.

If you are not sure about the interpretation of an object, look through the Word. It is rich with revelation and symbols. The Lord has been speaking to His people in dark sayings and symbols since the beginning of the world, and you are certain to find the answer to your revelation right in the Scriptures.

E. Vehicles

It is also common to interpret vehicles in your dreams as your ministry, specifically, the things that *drive* your ministry. You may dream that you are driving, but you are encountering difficulty. The Lord could be saying that you need to give Him the wheel and to stop taking your ministry out of His hands.

Perhaps you might dream that a person who symbolizes the Lord, is driving. In this case, it is a good interpretation, indicating that the Lord is in control and that you can relax for a while. Dreaming that your vehicle has broken down can speak of some kind of damage that you have faced in your ministry.

You could even dream that you receive keys to a new car! This speaks of promotion. The Lord could be confirming that He has given you a greater anointing to carry out the ministry He has given you.

F. Creatures/Animals

- Animals and insects can refer to demonic powers, but it also depends on how you view them.
- Plants and trees can refer to growth, or barrenness if they are in bad condition.
- Babies or children refer to things that have been birthed or are still immature.

Snakes, spiders, and black creatures in your dreams, very often speak of the enemy's work and his attacks.

A lion can speak of the Lord's strength. A lamb speaks of innocence and salvation. If you dream of your pet, you will need to identify what that pet means to you. Often pets are substitutes for children in which case they would represent a positive aspect of you.

G. Colors and Senses

- Things that were said or that you heard
- Things you felt, tasted, smelled

Often the color red can speak of the Lord's blood. Blue is a heavenly color, while black does not have a good connotation, as it is likened to the enemy's nature. In the Scriptures, gold often speaks of the Lord and His majesty, and silver speaks of humanity and redemption. Silver is also used when referring to finances.

White can speak of purity and green of fertility. Once again you would need to identify what they mean to you as an individual, as well as what they represent in the Word.

STEP 4: Get Revelation!

Once you have made your list and identified what each symbol represents, put the dream aside. Now, summarize what you receive from the Holy Spirit.

Write this final summary down. Don't flow from your intellect but use the internal anointing the Lord has given you for revelation.

Do not use the same formula on every dream you interpret. Allow the Holy Spirit to speak to you and give you additional visions and revelations to back up what you feel the dream means.

This is when you will give the person (or yourself) the direction and answers they are looking for. It is not good enough to just give an interpretation without following it up with the Word of God to encourage and promote faith, hope, and love.

If the dream indicates a warning, then add Scripture and direction on how to be victorious in that particular situation to the interpretation. If the dream is internal, guide the person through a better understanding of what is going on in their heart and show them how to move on from where they are.

If the dream is internal prophetic, then prepare them for the work the Lord is about to do in their lives.

If the dream is external, receive revelation from the Spirit and Word on what to do with the revelation. In other words, find out if it needs to be spoken forth as a decree, kept for a later time, travailed over in intercession, or shared with a group that you might intercede in unity with.

In Conclusion

James 5:1 says that if any man lacks wisdom all he needs to do is ask of the Lord and it will be given to him. So, ask and pray for wisdom! Daniel was known for the wisdom the Lord gave him with dreams. With the indwelling of the Holy Spirit, we also have that wisdom within us for every revelation and dream.

Receive that wisdom by faith and see the Lord open your eyes to a whole new realm of interpretation. As you allow yourself to be His vessel, He will open the way for you to use that gift and to bless the body of Christ with it.

I know that this chapter is pretty full and if dream interpretation is new to you, you might want to go over it a few times. So, do not be afraid to bookmark it and refer back to it. Even better, pick up *The Way of Dreams and Visions*[4] book and *Symbol Dictionary*[5] and go deeper into the study.

I pray that I gave you enough in this chapter though to already identify that your Savior has been talking to you nonstop! Can you see that? Wow! Think about it! Jesus loves you so much that not only did He reach out to you in your sleep, but He made sure to use pictures and symbols that you would understand.

Anyone else having that dream would not make sense of it. No, the Lord spoke secretly just to you. Are you beginning to realize just how precious you are to the Lord? By the end of this book, I pray that you take this one message away: The Lord Jesus desires to have an intimate relationship with you, and He died to make it a reality.

RAPID RECAP

1. *For most dreams, the symbols are a representation of your life.*
2. *Step 1: Categorize your dream*
3. *Step 2: Sense the spirit of your dream*
4. *Step 3: Identify each of the characters in your dream*
5. *Step 4: Put the pieces together using revelation*

#4 HEARING GOD THROUGH VISIONS

Ready to go deeper? I have shared each of the ways you can hear from the Lord in a very specific order, and I hope that as you dive into this chapter that you are already familiar with the language of the Word and also identify the Lord's love letters to you in your sleep.

Each way I have taught you so far has dug a deep foundation in your spiritual life and now... we go even deeper! Ready to hear from God on the run? Well, hearing Him through visions is simple and organic when you have fed the Word into your spirit.

Whenever I preach, I use the visions the Lord gives me. As I minister, I see pictures and then I explain them. It is very simple. The key is to be at peace. If you have fed enough Scripture into your spirit, it is very easy for those pictures to come back up when God wants to talk to you.

Now, if you didn't feed any Scripture into your spirit, will you still receive visions? Yes, the Lord will reach you in any way that you are available. However, if you do not have any Scripture in your spirit for Him to speak through, you will not understand the impressions and pictures that you see. You will have no point of reference. This will send you back to study to interpret every picture.

I's just better if you have a spirit full of the Word so that the Lord has lots of good stuff to give back to you when you need it.

PILLAR POINT:

If you are spiritually dry and have not fed on the Word, the flow of visions will dry up. This is especially true for people who have only studied theology and doctrine without spending time in the anointing.

Don't Be a Dry Cement Bag

They are like dry cement bags. They have houses upon houses of cement bags. When they try to flow in the spirit they cannot. This is because they have built their house out of cement bags, instead of combining the Word and Spirit.

What pictures did you put into your spirit? You study the dry logos and then cannot understand why you are not receiving visions or flowing in the spirit. It is because all you have pushed down is dry stuff without any pictures.

If you want to flow in the spirit, you need to put pictures from the Scriptures into your spirit.

What's a Vision?

> **2 Corinthians 12:1** *It is doubtless not profitable for me to boast. I will come to visions and revelations of the Lord.*

Paul was clearly used to receiving visions from the Lord. However, this way of hearing from Him is not restricted to the apostle. In fact, every believer can hear the Lord through visions. Prophets tend to flow in it more than most.

I thrive on visions! Whether I am preaching, playing a song, singing in the spirit, walking down the road, talking to the Lord... I live in visions.

So, what's a vision? Let me make it plain.

PILLAR POINT:

A vision is simply a picture in your mind.

What I love about visions is that they give you the next step along the road. The Word says that He is a lamp for our feet and a light on our path.

Visions are like the lamp by your foot. Visions do not give you the full picture all at once.

When the Lord gives you revelation, He gives it to you a piece at a time. He doesn't offload the whole thing on you at once. It comes a piece at a time. He will give you one little picture, and as you share that piece, you will receive more.

You can experience visions in your private times with the Lord, whether you are praying, reading, talking, or just submitting the day to Him. You can be sensitive to the pictures that He puts into your mind.

This is the language of heaven. The Lord speaks in pictures. Learn to identify them in every aspect of your life.

When the Lord uses your sense of sight to speak to you, you receive a vision. He is sending you a picture from your spirit. That is why most visions you receive come from deep within.

The pictures and words you receive are impulses and deep impressions. They are gentle and flow as rivers of living water.

How Visions Work

> *Mark 4:33 And with many such **parables** He spoke the word to them, as they were able to hear [it].*

When Jesus walked the earth, He spoke in parables and pictures to illustrate His point. He hasn't changed since. He still loves to give us pictures. Why? We remember pictures.

It is hard to remember a prophetic word, but it is easy to remember an illustration. Let's be honest, you and I are both still thinking about the house that almost fell apart that I spoke about at the beginning of this book.

The Lord will do the same. He will put pictures in your mind and use visions to speak to you. Hearing Him in this way is something you can continually develop.

It is great to go on impressions, or the audible voice, but without visions, you are a blind man.

Visions are like taking a snapshot with a camera. It tells the story. You know, I could try to explain to you what a rose looks like, or I could take a picture so you can see the colors yourself.

What is going to be more effective? Well, it's the same in the spirit. You can understand the Word and get impressions from your spirit, but when you see visions, it puts it all into place.

So, visions are a very important way of being able to hear God's voice. Do you flow in visions? If so, develop it! Let it become the most important thing to you.

If you are not there yet, then do not be discouraged! It is quite likely that you are flowing in this way already but don't realize it.

The Three Vision Categories

1st Category: Prophetic Visions

> *John 7:38 He who believes in Me, as the Scripture has said, out of his heart will flow **rivers** of living **water.***

The Holy Spirit uses the vision category of prophetic visions often to speak to His people. Hearing God in this way feels like what the passage above describes.

These visions flow out from deep within, like rivers of water. For many people, this is the most difficult concept to grasp, even though it is the easiest to master.

In fact, the Lord Jesus is speaking to you all the time via impressions and visions. You just do not recognize this. Many prophets who have come to our ministry for training, have struggled with this.

They were so used to hearing from the Lord externally, that they waited for their visions to be suspended or to fall into a trance before they said, "I received a vision from God!" Sure, God speaks in this way also, but it is not the primary method He uses.

Unfortunately, many have sought these experiences and have certainly found them... but not all can be accredited to the Holy Spirit!

Have you ever wondered why deception is running rampant in the prophetic ministry? It is because believers are continuously *searching* for the open vision.

Rest assured that God is speaking to you through visions. It is the most articulate language of the Spirit, because sight is our strongest sense.

He speaks today like He did to Apostle Paul when he saw a Macedonian inviting him to come and preach to them. The Macedonian was a symbol of the people God was sending him to.

I cover interpreting symbols in your visions in my book, *The Way of Dreams and Visions*[6], so I won't belabor the point here.

Rather, I want to draw your attention to the fact that you are already hearing God. Do you know those *impressions* you have been receiving when praying? Those are visions!

However, when you expect to go into a trance, or for the Lord to *slam* you with an open vision, you miss the fact that you could be having a conversation with the Lord every moment of your day.

Visions are simple pictures that come from your spirit, leaving an impression on your mind. You might be praying with someone when you might see a picture in your mind of a river that is blocked. That is a vision!

When you *get it* that you have been seeing visions all along, a whole new world will open up to you. Then you can focus on that and expect it. You will discover that God has been talking to you all along.

PILLAR POINT:

Prophetic visions are pictorial impressions that come to your mind from your spirit.

2nd Category: Trance Visions

Acts 11:5 I was in the city of Joppa praying; and in a trance I saw a vision, an object descending like a great sheet, let down from heaven by four corners; and it came to me.

Our second category of visions is the kind Peter had while waiting for lunch to be ready. This is a vision where your senses are suspended. You suddenly smell, feel, or see things in the spirit that you don't feel in the natural.

Your eyes are closed, and it feels as if you are somewhere else. John G. Lake certainly operated in this very strongly. It's no surprise because he was an evangelist. He would pray for someone from a long distance and see them being healed in the spirit, even though he was not there.

The Scripture above records one of the very few instances where this type of vision is mentioned. This makes one think... When you consider the message of this vision, I understand why the Lord gave Peter a trance instead of a simple prophetic vision.

Consider that in this vision Peter even struggled with the Lord. He really did not want to hear this message! He tried to denounce it, but it was so strong, he had to pay attention.

Had the Lord tried to give Peter this message as a prophetic vision, he might have brushed it aside as his *imagination* and not thought about it further. However, God really had a point to make.

He had to work through Peter's prejudice and open his eyes to an entirely new secret about the New Testament church. Never once did it occur to Peter that salvation was also for the Gentiles... not until that vision!

So, clearly God needed to make a point. I would daresay that those who function in this vision type often are ones God is really trying to get a message across to.

PILLAR POINT:

In a trance vision, the Lord suspends your senses, because He needs you to put your own ideas aside and listen to Him.

This is what Zechariah found out when he decided to argue with the angel who told him that he would be John the Baptist's father. The Lord made such a point, He struck him mute!

So, if you have flowed in this kind of vision, take note! The Lord has a strong message for you that you are meant to obey. If you do not flow in this way, then you can take a deep breath of relief. Perhaps you are ready to hear God and won't *brush aside* His message, so He does not have to suspend your senses!

3rd Category: Open Visions

> *Numbers 24:4 The utterance of him who hears the words of God, who sees the **vision** of the Almighty, who falls down, with eyes wide **open***:

You will notice that open visions are rarely mentioned and only in the Old Testament. There are a number of reasons for this. The first is that the Holy Spirit was not indwelling in the Old Testament.

When God spoke to man, He had to do so externally. He appeared when He willed and only for short periods of time. In the New Testament, we can hear God any time we need to.

Just imagine, in the Old Testament they did not have the luxury of an internal Urim and Thummim. They had to schlep all the way to the high priest to hear from God.

They also had to wait for the Lord to come upon them if they wanted to hear Him through visions. Well, in the passage above, we observe quite an interesting occurrence. What makes it interesting is that Balaam was a false prophet!

Balaam

In fact, he opened his mouth, ready to curse Israel and in that moment, God stepped in and took over. Instead of speaking that curse, God superimposed a completely different picture over his eyes as he looked over the tents of Israel.

In other words, his eyes were open, but what he saw was not the reality, but a picture God wanted him to see.

PILLAR POINT:

In an open vision, a picture is superimposed over your natural senses. Your eyes see what God wants them to see (such as in the case of Balaam).

The Lord literally took Balaam over to make sure that His perfect will was spoken forth instead of the curse.

I think it stands to reason that if God has to take you over and shout at you so loudly... that you are not terribly open to hearing His voice but have your own agenda.

I am not saying God does not speak in this way today. He is God! He can do what He pleases. I am saying that in our New Testament era, He does not need to shout as He did in the past.

He does not need to wait for the right moment to come upon us and bend us to His will. He speaks to us from within. He has filled us with rivers of living water, and so He will flow out from within.

It is quite possible that the Lord might use this kind of vision in an environment where the person He is speaking to needs to get it right down to the letter.

However, this is not normally the realm of the prophet. So, if you can flow more in prophetic visions, you will find your ministry leaping to the next level.

What if Your Trance and Open Visions Stopped?

If you have been flowing in trance and open visions and then they stopped, do not be concerned! The Lord is not ignoring you. In fact, I daresay that you got the message and are now open to hearing Him without Him having to shout.

I wish that I could say the same about Balaam though. He was so stubborn God made his donkey prophesy!

New Testament Difference

The indwelling of the Holy Spirit has changed everything. Before, only a select few could hear Him. Now the Scripture says:

> **Acts 2:17** *And it shall come to pass in the last days, says God, that I will pour out of My spirit on all flesh; your sons and your daughters shall prophesy, your young men shall see* **visions***, your old men shall dream* **dreams***:*

The Spirit of God is now poured out on us all! Every single one of us can hear from God.

Hopefully this has given you a good picture of what visions are and how to flow in them. They are a powerful way to hear the Lord's voice and once you master this, the other four ways I will teach on will build upon that foundation.

Before signing off on this chapter, let me mention briefly that if you flowed in external signs, open and trans visions and they suddenly stopped, it could also well be that God is moving you from the evangelistic to the prophetic ministry.

You did not fail the Lord. He is training you to function in a different way and to minister to His people in a new way. This is good news! Embrace this evolution in your spiritual life and recognize that this shift is not a sign of failure, but of promotion.

RAPID RECAP

1. *Visions are pictures that come from your spirit and are imprinted on your mind.*
2. *God will speak through visions using parables.*
3. *There are three main vision categories. Prophetic, trance, and open visions.*
4. *Often trance and open visions are given for a message that is hard to receive or requires a firm hand from God.*
5. *The indwelling of the Holy Spirit enables every believer to flow in visions.*

#5 HEARING GOD THROUGH TONGUES AND UTTERANCE

1 Corinthians 14:18 I thank my God I speak with tongues more than you all.

I have had many opportunities in my life to learn different languages. In the country I grew up in, there were eleven official languages. Depending on where you lived, you would learn that region's tribal language.

Unfortunately, we moved around a lot, so I never really got to learn any of these languages properly. We moved every six months. Just when I started to learn a bit of one language, we would move, and I had to start all over.

I must admit, as a result I had some pretty bad thoughts on learning a language. It seemed really hard for me because I could never get the hang of it.

When I went into ministry and the Lord moved us to the opposite end of the world, I had to learn again. Now I was in a Spanish-speaking world and I had to learn Spanish... at least enough to say, "Hey, where is the bathroom?"

After I got over my bad past experiences and fears, it became a lot of fun.

I think it is pretty clear for everyone who is learning a language for the first time that it is not always easy. It is exciting though when you finally get it right.

I experienced this for the first time in Europe after I had finally learned to speak a bit of German. I went to Germany and had my first full conversation with a stranger I met there.

Okay, sure... I was asking him about the chicken and how much it cost, but the point was that I could ask it in his native tongue. Even better... he actually understood me! It was so exciting! It lit a fire in me. I was now able to communicate to a whole new world of people. Suddenly, languages became an exciting experience.

Flowing in Tongues

When it comes to the world of the Spirit there is also a language we have to learn, and it is called speaking in tongues. I tell you what is exciting about speaking in tongues though: You don't have to go through all that tough learning. You don't have to get books and audio-visuals.

It is a gift that we receive in the Spirit. Nonetheless, just like I had to learn German to be able to communicate with a German speaking person, it is the same with this. If you want to understand the realm of the Spirit and its messages, you need to speak its language. That language is called the gift of tongues.

This is a very special gift. It is not just about speaking the right things. This gift has the power to tap into your spirit and do things in your spiritual life that you probably haven't even begun to develop yet.

I think that especially with people like me who grew up in a charismatic, Pentecostal environment, speaking in tongues was the first thing you did. Craig learned about speaking in tongues right after he came to know the Lord.

It can become so commonplace that you really lose the power it has to transform your life.

In my opinion, this is one of the most important gifts that you need to flow in. It is the starting point of all the other gifts of the Spirit.

I won't get into doctrinal controversy here and say that you are not saved if you cannot speak in tongues. I don't think that we need to take it and make a *god* out of it. Simply put, without the gift of tongues you have a serious lack in your spiritual life.

It is like lacking the power of the atom bomb and instead trying to use a little pea-shooter against the enemy.

Speaking in tongues gives you the power you need to tap into the realm of the Spirit. Not only that, but it also gives you the power to release what you have received from the Lord in the spirit.

Purpose for Speaking in Tongues

As you speak in tongues, you get rid of all the junk you put into your spirit and you feed it instead. Once you have fed your spirit you will have enough anointing to pour out to everyone around you.

You really need to take that time. It is like a chef who spends all his time cooking and preparing food. There comes a time when he has to sit down and eat.

You need to take the time in your spiritual walk to stop and feed your spirit so that you can effectively feed others.

If you don't take time to charge up, there is a danger that you just carry on doing what you have always done and as a result, your revelation will come from your mind.

You won't feel the anointing any longer and this is probably the biggest problem of all. You begin lacking the anointing and it is because you aren't taking the time to tap into your spirit.

I hope I am challenging you back to basics. What is the core purpose of speaking in tongues?

1. Builds Your Spirit Up

Firstly, speaking in tongues builds up your spirit. I had a couple of bodybuilders in my family on my mother's side. In fact, right into his older years, my grandfather was a keen weight training fanatic.

He and my uncles were big strong guys with bulging muscles. When we went on vacation or he stayed at our house during holidays, instead of sleeping in like the rest of us, my grandfather was usually up at six or seven in the morning, pumping weights in the gym.

I thought to myself, "That's the craziest thing. You are supposed to be taking a break. You are supposed to be chilling out." But there he was... at the gym.

But you know... that's why he looked the way he did. He was always building up his muscles. If ever he had to stop, he would have lost those muscles, power, and strength.

Tap Into Your Inner Bodybuilder!

Well, it is the same in the spirit. You need to ask yourself, "Is there a spiritual bodybuilder inside of me, or a weedy little nerd?"

Well, that depends on how much you have been building your spirit up. Don't think that because a year ago you were this big muscular, tough guy in the spirit that you are still there now.

Unless you maintain it on a regular basis, you will lose that edge. When you put the effort in, you reap the fruit of it.

Do you want a nice, strong, muscular spirit? Then you need to continue speaking in tongues and make it part of your daily life. Then you will be that big, spiritual bodybuilder who is strong and muscular, ready to take on anything that comes your way.

2. Cleanses Your Spirit

One of the most exciting things about tongues and probably its most practical use, is that it cleans out your spirit fast!

This is a powerful principle that is easily forgotten. You get so busy striving and trying to please the Lord that you get distracted. You forget that there is a simple way to get back into His presence and bring your spirit in line.

You can get spiritually fit again by just taking time to speak in tongues.

Have you been distracted? Perhaps you have had a tough week and all hell has broken loose against you. Speaking in tongues gives you the life you need.

Perhaps you are frustrated and battling to hear the Lord's voice. You think to yourself, "Was that the Lord or was this my imagination again?"

Speaking in tongues brings your spirit to life. It separates the dross from the gold. It separates the spirit from the flesh like oil and water.

Sometimes things can look a little bit mixed up and you don't know what's the flesh and what's the spirit. Speaking in tongues brings that clear division.

Speaking in tongues is like drilling through rock to sink a pipe into an underground stream for the purpose of setting up a windmill. Once the windmill is all set up, the wind just needs to blow, and the living water will spring up from the ground.

Getting to that point takes a bit of effort though. The best way to make sure you have God's fresh water on tap is by speaking in tongues for long periods of time.

Setting up Your Windmill

Perhaps your pipe has gotten a little bit clogged along the line. It got a bit jammed up with stress, the fight you had with your spouse, the struggles you have at work, and the conflicts you have at church. Through it all, you get plugged up and contaminated.

At first you don't realize it, but then you notice that you lost *the edge* when you minister. Don't think that your spirit is always just free because you are in ministry all the time.

Sometimes you can get so hung up on doing the work of the ministry and on pouring out that you get clogged up and dull in your spirit. You forget to tap into the life source.

If you have been running around and ministering to others, pouring out of your portion, chances are that after a while you will feel a little dry.

You will start pouring out from your intellect and you will rely on what you know in your head. You won't give people the life force of the Spirit that is inside of you and will swap it out for a bunch of rotten manna.

Speaking in tongues changes all of that. Firstly, it gets your mind out the way, because you are not concentrating on all the cares and problems and trying to come up with logical solutions. Secondly, it taps into the stream of life inside of you.

Speaking in tongues is one of the best ways to tap into that anointing and to make sure that what you speak comes gushing out with fresh (spiritual) water.

Utterance

> *1 Corinthians 14:5 I wish you all spoke with tongues, but even more that you prophesied; for he who prophesies is greater than he who speaks with tongues, unless indeed he interprets, that the church may receive edification.*

You can't always speak in tongues though. You also have to speak in your native language to fully understand what God is saying to you.

It is great when you get together with a bunch of believers and carry on in tongues for hours. You can all have a wonderful time and share in the presence of the Lord.

However, even Apostle Paul said in the passage above, "Guys, if you are in a public meeting, if you speak in tongues, you have to speak out the utterance! You have to speak it in the native tongue, so that everybody can be edified, and the Lord can reveal what is in their hearts."

It is a fantastic opportunity to practice this in a local church. If you are new to utterance and interpretation though, the best way for you to get into the flow is to do so in your prayer closet.

In fact, this is the way I learned to interpret my own tongues. I learned in the privacy of my prayer closet, where the pile of laundry I had yet to pack away, was the only recipient to bear the brunt of my mistakes.

The Difference Between Utterance and Interpretation

Before I speak more about how to flow in utterance, let me briefly clarify the difference between utterance and interpretation. The secret lies in the following passage:

> *1 Corinthians 14:27 If anyone speaks in a tongue, let there be two or at the most three, each in turn, and let one interpret.*

PILLAR POINT:

To put it plainly, an utterance is a flow of inspired tongues that comes from your spirit.
An Interpretation is the interpretation of those tongues into your native language.

Perhaps you have seen this take place in a meeting. Growing up, this was my norm. Someone would stand up during worship and belt out a confident string of inspired tongues. A strong silence followed as everyone wondered, "Who will bring the interpretation?"

Then, everyone breathed a sigh of relief as the usual guy got up and interpreted. The sigh of relief stemmed from, "Whew! I am glad the guy speaking out that utterance did not miss it!" or, "Whew I am glad that God did not call on me to bring the interpretation!"

Learning to Flow in Utterance and Interpretation

The key is to practice this in your private prayer time first. Don't feel pressured that you have to be a big hotshot out there.

You can practice this in your quiet time with the Lord and learn to develop this ability in a safe place. Prophesy over yourself. Prophesy over your children. Speak in tongues and pray for people you know well. Develop it! Take your time and become familiar with this language of the Spirit.

When I first started learning German, I wasn't so arrogant as to think that I could hold a whole conversation with the two German words I knew.

Some people are that arrogant and they are annoying. I didn't want to be annoying. I wanted to make sure I could at least speak a sentence.

I suggest you do the same with the language of the Spirit. Learn a bit! Take time to get to know the realm of the Spirit, and the Lord's voice.

Then, when you step out you will do so with confidence. You will have good experiences, not bad ones that will leave you feeling discouraged.

Step by Step Interpretation

The best part about practicing this in private is that it is alright to mess up! We put way too much pressure on ourselves as believers. We put a level of perfection on our spiritual life, that God never did.

The Lord is patient with you, so be patient with yourself, okay? Trying this for yourself is simple.

Come into the presence of the Lord and worship or pray until you feel the anointing. I suggest taking time to just speak in tongues.

Then ask the Lord for the interpretation and open your mouth and speak the first words in your native tongue that come to your mind. Is that the Lord? Well, you will only know when you step out!

When God is speaking, you will feel an anointing and you will not be able to keep up. Do you remember the first time you spoke in tongues? I don't know how it was for you, but when I got Spirit-filled, I could hardly keep up! I had to grab a quick breath because I felt like I was on a freight train. The Holy Spirit had a lot to say!

Flowing in utterance and interpretation is received the same way you receive the gift of tongues or salvation. It takes faith and a decision to step out. So, go ahead! At first you might stumble over your words and feel awkward. That is alright, you keep stepping out until you feel that shift.

From there... the sky is the limit!

Sing in Tongues

A fantastic way to learn to interpret your tongues is to praise and worship in tongues during your private times with God.

If you want to take your spiritual life up a notch, try singing your tongues while playing an instrument (guitar, piano, etc.), or perhaps while you are driving your kids to school (if they can bear it).

Also, take the time to interpret your tongues while you are singing. It is a fantastic first step to learning how to prophesy in song.

I learned to do this a very long time ago. I can't remember the exact date I started because it has been such an integral part of my life and ministry.

Every time you lead worship, there will be something new! The Lord will give you a new song and new wisdom. So, give that a try! You will be amazed at the sudden increase in anointing.

There is just something about music. When you combine tongues, music, and interpretation there is such power. Give it a try in your next prayer time and soon you will be raving about it as much as I am.

Tongues, utterance, and interpretation are powerful ways to hear God's voice and the more time you spend in the Word and in the Spirit, the more you can expect to hear God in this way.

Once you are familiar with this, flowing in prophecy and moving onto journaling will be a natural progression. Although I won't teach you how to hear God's voice through prophecy in this book, I cover it in some detail in the *Prophetic Functions*[7] book. Instead, I will go directly to hearing God through journaling which combines the *how to* of interpretation and prophecy beautifully.

RAPID RECAP

1. *The gift of tongues builds up your spirit.*
2. *Speaking in tongues cleanses your spirit of all the garbage you fed into it.*
3. *Utterance is the interpretation of tongues into your native language.*
4. *The best place to practice tongues and interpretation is at home, over yourself.*
5. *Singing in tongues and then singing the interpretation increases the anointing.*
6. *Speak out the first English words that come to your mind.*
7. *Don't be afraid to practice and perfect this ability.*

#6 HOW TO HEAR GOD THROUGH JOURNALING

1 Chronicles 28:19 *"All this," said David, "the Lord made me understand in writing, by His hand upon me, all the works of these plans."*

O ne of the first things I taught my children was how to have a conversation. You would think that this is something natural to us humans, but it really is not!

Children aren't born knowing how to have a good conversation. In fact, usually kids are very one-sided in their conversation. They are all about "look at me" and talk about everything they did. If you have hung out with my eleven-year-old son long enough, you will leave having learned about every breed of dinosaur and fun facts about the life of the honey badger. (The Lord alone knows why of all God's creatures these are his favorite!)

I had to teach him that perhaps not everyone he meets has the passion to learn the difference between dinosaurs and prehistoric animals. Conversation lessons were essential to surviving public ministry life!

And so, as I did with each of my daughters, I also had to teach Michael the social skill of having a conversation. I taught him to ask things like, "How are you?"

"You look lovely today!"

"How many children do you have?"

I realized that conversation is an art. I only saw the fruit of this when my daughters were a little older. I bumped into a new neighbor who had met my kids before me.

The lady said, "I was so amazed. Your kids showed an interest in the kind of person I am. I never met children like that before. They came into my home and said, 'Wow, you've got such a lovely home. How long have you lived here?'"

She said, "They asked questions that children just never ask, and it was such a pleasure to have a conversation with them."

Can I just say… #ProudMomMoment!

The Art of Journaling

Journaling is just like learning how to develop a conversation.

PILLAR POINT:

Simply put, journaling is having a written conversation with the Lord.

You approach Him with your thoughts and ideas, and then write down what He tells you.

He might speak to you in visions, or you might hear His still, small voice. It is comparable to operating in utterance or prophecy, just that you write down what you would say out loud.

What It Looks Like

Here is a journaling example for you:

"Lord, I am having another bad day. I did not get any sleep last night because the kids kept me up and I still have not done my laundry. I do not feel like getting out of bed today, Lord."

Then you give the Lord a chance to talk.

The Secret to Hearing

That is one of the secrets to hearing His voice. You have to be real with Him and say it like it is. Come to Him as you are. Write down all your pitiful woes, how sad you are, and whatever else is going on. Then quieten your spirit.

At this point, a picture, memory, or Scripture might come to mind. Now simply write it down. Don't write it in third person, but first person, directly from the Lord.

To summarize, after I have written my part, I close my eyes and say, "Lord, what do you have to tell me?" Then, I might see a picture of a river meandering through an open field that is lush, green, and beautiful. How do I vocalize that?

It might look a little like this:

"It is time to come into my rest, my child. Come and sit by the water and rest beside the river because you have been surrounded by so much chaos. It is time to put your problems aside and to come into my presence to sit by the stream for a little while."

You are journaling! It takes a little bit of practice and for the first while, it will probably be straight from your mind. Relax!

It is okay. It is not like you have committed the unpardonable sin by hearing from your mind and not from God.

It Is Okay to Mess Up

It does not have to be perfect from the start. Have you ever heard a child learning to speak? My son, Michael, couldn't say "Denise" when he was three years old. He said, "Neese" instead. He could not speak full sentences. He said things like:

"I come with."

"Hot tea, please (which really sounded more like, 'hot tea, pwease!')"

He could not pronounce the letter "l" correctly at first, but after a while, he got the words right. When he first started saying "ma ma" or "da da", I did not say, "Would you please say, mother, father, sister, brother… and can I hear you quote the books of the Bible please?"

No, give the guy a break! He was just learning to speak. He got there in time. Just like a baby needs time to learn to speak, we need time to learn to hear God's voice correctly. Yes, some of what you write down will be your thoughts and ideas.

However, the more you do it, the better you will get at discerning the difference. You will look back over older journals and see the parts that were God and the parts that were you. The more you get used to hearing His voice, the more you will recognize where you are getting off track.

It is a process. It is a relationship. Even in a marriage relationship, it takes a while to understand what the other person is *really* saying. It takes time to get to know one another. It is the same with the Lord.

Your Upbringing Conditions You

Unfortunately, there are a lot of preconceived ideas that you have from growing up in the church. Most of the skills we have in getting along with people come from the home.

The kind of relationship you had with your parents and siblings will determine how well you can have a conversation.

So, you come to the Lord, ready to share your heart and hear His voice but find yourself in a bind.

The problem is that you have so many ideas in your mind about how you should be approaching God and how you should be talking to Him that you are hindered in your ability to journal.

If you want to get more instruction on how to journal please read, *The Way of Dreams and Visions*[8], *Practical Prophetic Ministry*[9] or *Called to the Ministry*[10].

RAPID RECAP

1. *Journaling is a written conversation between you and the Lord.*
2. *Approach journaling with a question.*
3. *Do not stop halfway to look up Scriptures.*
4. *Journal often to see the revelation progress.*

9

DO'S AND DON'TS
OF JOURNALING

I want to take a quick look at the do's and don'ts for journaling. Pick up pen and paper, as they are very practical.

You may already know what should be done, but why be satisfied with what you have? There is always room to go deeper!

1. Listen

Take time to hear what God has to say. You might be thinking, "That's a no-brainer! We are talking about journaling after all!" You would be surprised how many people are so busy talking to the Lord about their problems that they never stop to hear what He has to say.

Remember what I shared about how I taught my children to ask questions and to listen for the answer? That is such a vital part of journaling. Listen to what He wants to say. Don't get too self-absorbed!

It could be that the Lord wants to talk about something completely different. He may want to answer your question in a way you do not expect. I have experienced this many times in my journals.

Listen to what God has to say! Don't get so wrapped up in your ideas that the Lord literally shouts at you through the journal! Don't keep pulling Him back to your point.

2. Make Your Request Clear

Furthermore, make your request clear. Approach the Lord with a clear purpose for your journal. This helps to give your journal a direction.

If you just want to hear His voice then say, "Lord, what do you have to say to me today? What is your direction for me today?"

Come with an idea of what you will say because it is a conversation. Say to the Lord, "Lord, this is my need and care," or, "Hey, how are you doing? I just want to hear what you have to say."

This gives you a clear track to run on. Once you get the conversation rolling, the Lord will develop it from there.

3. Be Real and Honest

When I want to go out with a good friend, I don't say, "It would please me to have you accompany me to the nearest coffee shop, so that we might share a tasty beverage. Would you extend me the grace by accepting my eager invitation?"

So, it stands to reason that I don't talk in theatrical language and religious speech to the Lord either.

I might simply say to my friend, "Hey, how is it going? You want to come around for a cup of coffee?"

Well, Jesus is your best friend, and you should be more real and honest with Him than with any other person in this world.

You don't have to approach the Lord in a formatted, formal way.

By all means, have a healthy fear of the Father. It is important to have reverence, because He is God.

However, the kind of relationship I am talking about here is an intimate relationship with the Lord Jesus.

The exciting thing is, when you are real and honest with Him, He is very real and honest with you. The Lord Jesus will always meet you at your relationship boundary line. He is a gentleman.

PILLAR POINT:

Are you looking for a straight answer to something? Then ask Him a straight question.

Don't word your question in a way that sounds nicer than the reality. He knows what's in your heart anyway.

Say it like it is. Say it how you feel it. Say what you really think.

If you feel embarrassed about how it really is, delete the journal afterwards, okay? (If that makes you feel any better.)

This is a good starting point to making your journals come alive and experiencing the real person of Christ. Your honesty will provoke honest answers back.

4. Do Not Paste in Tons of Scriptures

Under no circumstance should you paste in hundreds of Scriptures. What's the point?

That is like having a conversation with a friend and you are trying to back up every statement with a Scripture.

I hate to break it to you, but the Lord already knows what He said in the Word. He originated it. He doesn't need to quote it back at Himself.

I see this so often with those called to be prophets. They paste Scripture references into their journals just to back up what the Lord said. However, the speech of the Word should be natural.

The Language of God

As the Lord speaks to you in your journals, He will say things like, "My child, I have called you to be the head and not the tail, above and not beneath."

However, He won't add the disclaimer, "Please go to Deuteronomy 28:44…" He knows where it is. He doesn't need to repeat it and He doesn't need to back Himself up.

Try to get away from it because if you get into the *I have to go look up all the Scriptures* mode, you cut the flow of your spirit and get into your mind. That is when you start walking a delicate line that can even lead to deception.

By overanalyzing what God is saying, you give the enemy the opening he needs to get his ideas in there.

If you are unsure about the content of your journal, simply look up the Scriptures afterwards.

5. Do Not Use Theological Spiritual Language

From what I have seen over the years, many believers seem to think that the Lord speaks in King James English.

Here is a newsflash: He doesn't! In fact, you will find that Jesus was rather ordinary. So much so that the Pharisees needed Judas to identify Him. He looked ordinary and used ordinary language.

Of course, the authority He spoke with was extraordinary! Surely the power those words were spoken with was not ordinary!

He spoke in such a way that the uneducated beggars understood Him. Prostitutes understood Him.

When He had Nicodemus over for dinner, He had to say, "For somebody who is so educated, you really don't have a clue" (John 3:10)! He was talking so plainly that Nicodemus in his theological, spiritual understanding could not understand the simplicity of His message.

He Talks My Language!

> PILLAR POINT:
>
> When you experience an intimate relationship with Jesus you will realize that He speaks your language. He speaks like you speak.

If you speak French, He speaks French. If you speak English, He speaks English. He speaks to you in a way that you understand.

The Lord doesn't speak in reverential whispers and He certainly doesn't speak in King James English. He speaks in pictures, types, and shadows.

6. Do Not Use Jargon and Spiritual Buzzwords

There are so many *Christian buzzwords* floating around in the church. There are terms we have grown up with or have received from other ministries.

And so, you just copy them without a second thought.

However, you don't stop to look in the Scriptures for yourself. These buzzwords end up becoming a doctrine because no one took the time to look them up.

So, watch out for these little terms! Especially the common terms that are out there but aren't based on the Word.

You do not need to get paranoid. There are definitely some good ones that are based on the Word. The Lord will use them to illustrate His point. He will talk about named principles that you have studied to make a point.

Where Did It Originate?

This is just one of my little personal pet peeves. You can either take it with a pinch of salt, or take it as a challenge and say, "Yes, that's a good point. Why do I always say that? Where did I get that buzzword from?"

Perhaps you have a few that come to your mind. Here are a few I hear often:

"New level, new devil."

"Name it and claim it, brother!"

"If it's His will, it's His bill!"

"Too blessed to be stressed!"

"God is good all the time. All the time, God is good!"

If you want to journal and enter into an intimate relationship with the Lord, you need to cut through meaningless conversation.

You will need to cut through the religious mindsets. Cut out the fancy language, and the misconceptions and your relationship with the Lord will become real, alive, and evolve into something wonderful.

Here is a tip to help you identify a buzzword: Would you use that in a normal conversation?

Final Challenge

So, what are you going to do? Will you take up the challenge or will you say, "No, my journals are great. I have got it all together. I think it is pretty perfect!"

Have you developed the art of conversation with the Lord to the point where you are so comfortable talking to Him and hearing what He has to say in response?

Are your journals still in point form, or do they look like a conversation? They should look as if somebody took the conversation and transcribed it.

It takes time to get it right. I know that as you apply yourself, you will soon come to the place where you are talking face to face with Jesus!

10

#7 HEARING GOD THROUGH THE AUDIBLE AND STILL SMALL VOICE

The Audible Voice

> **Acts 22:7** *And I fell to the ground and heard a voice saying to me, 'Saul, Saul, why are you persecuting Me?'*

You can also hear the Lord through the audible voice. This is not as common, but Moses must have heard the Lord in this way.

When somebody can only hear the audible voice though and doesn't flow in any of the other ways, I question it.

I question it because if they can only hear the audible voice, but don't receive visions, can't journal, and can't hear the Lord personally, then I wonder what voice they are hearing. Is it really the Lord's voice?

If the Lord has to shout all the time, you either do not know how to listen, or the voice you are hearing is not God's and is drowning out the still, small voice from within.

God is talking twenty-four hours a day! You just need to listen. When I journal, worship, or speak in tongues, I get visions, and an Urim or Thummim. The moment I get into His presence, the revelation flows automatically.

So, if somebody can only hear an audible voice but doesn't hear the Lord in any other way, I am suspicious and want to test that spirit.

This would fall into the same category as an open vision. Yes, God is well able to speak in this way and He chooses to at times. However, it is not the only way through which He speaks to His people.

You cannot tell the church that the only way they can hear God for themselves is to wait for an audible voice to come from the sky.

Hearing God's audible voice has often happened to those who needed a clear confirmation of their salvation. It likely happened when they got born again or maybe it was even the reason for their salvation. A good scriptural example of this is Apostle Paul on his way to Damascus.

The Lord had to stop him dead in his tracks. Accompanying that voice was a blinding light and a backhander, knocking him to the ground!

Fortunately for us all, Paul got the message pretty quickly. The Lord did not have to resort to such extreme measures again to get through to him!

The Still Small Voice

> *1 Corinthians 3:16 Do you not know that you are the temple of God and that the Spirit of God dwells in you?*

From the time we are born again, the Holy Spirit comes to dwell within us. The still, small voice is by far one of the most common ways to hear Him.

In fact, it is likely you have heard this voice often, but have just not recognized it. Often, we look for the loud voice, not realizing that Jesus is a gentleman.

That is certainly what Elijah experienced when he was running away from Jezebel in 1 Kings 19:12. He expected to hear the Lord in the earthquake, but instead heard Him in the gentle breeze.

This is a beautiful picture of what the Lord had in mind for us all along. As believers, we have the Holy Spirit within, and so that breeze is always blowing. You will hear it during times when you are crying out for an answer or when it is time to take a new direction.

How Do You Know if It's God?

When I am feeling weary, He lifts my arms from behind and says, "Push on through. You can do it."

The inner voice is the Lord speaking to you via your own spirit. In fact, it is a lot like receiving a vision, only that it is words that are formed in your mind instead of a picture.

It Will Sound Like You

So, how do you know if you are making things up or if it is really the Lord? The first time I became aware of this voice, I was sure I was making things up. It happened to me when I met Craig for the first time.

We were working as waiters in a popular restaurant and so we bumped into one another during a work shift. As we met, I heard a voice in my spirit say, "Be careful how you handle this meeting, because this could be your future husband."

I thought I was hearing things. Well, the Lord knew that I needed a little help because the road I was determined to walk on at that time had me going in a very different direction to the way God wanted me to go!

PILLAR POINT:

When you first start paying attention to that inner voice, it starts off with a feeling, of *yes, no,* or *maybe*. As you develop it more and practice His presence more, you hear a soft thought.

It will be a thought that sounds like you but is coming from your spirit.

The thought might say, "I love you."

"I would prefer it if you did not do that."

"I do not think this is a good idea."

"I really think you should go for that."

You may not even be able to vocalize it word for word at the beginning.

It Will Be Gentle

The still small voice will be an array of thoughts, but not pushy thoughts. It will be gentle. Learn to hear His voice through the other six ways before you attempt this one.

The enemy will try to interject pushy thoughts in your mind. You will need to know the Lord's voice well before listening in this way.

You have probably experienced this already. You find yourself in a crisis situation that is really tough, or dangerous. In the midst of it, you suddenly get this thought that everything will be okay.

It does not even make sense because in the natural, everything is falling apart. The bills are due, the finances are not coming in, but you get this thought that everything will be okay, and the rent will be paid.

You think, "Where did that thought come from?"

When you start realizing that those thoughts are the Lord's voice and you link them to the Urim and Thummim you have been feeling, and the Word you have been pushing down, guess what happens?

Pictures start to build. You realize that God has been trying to tell you something all along. That is the wonderful thing about hearing the Lord's voice.

He does not only speak one way. He does not give you a prophetic word and that is it.

He will speak through the Urim and Thummim, through visions, and also through your journals.

Practicing His Presence Project

It will take time to really get to know Him. From there, you will start hearing the still, small voice. The best way to develop hearing the still, small voice, is to practice His presence.

This is a very simple project. Everywhere you go, realize that Jesus is there with you. So, when I am preaching, I am imagining the Lord standing right next to me. He gives me notes every now and again. He gives me a squeeze on the shoulder every now and again and says, "You are doing great. Hang in there!"

When I am feeling weary, He gets my back saying, "Push on through! You can do it!"

He says, "Hey, did you think about this?" I see Him right there and I sense His presence with me.

Then we go to lunch and I imagine the Lord sitting with me. Then He says, "Watch this!" I see the conversation turn. One person says something that sparks the next person off. Next thing you know, we are having church in the middle of a busy restaurant!

Then we have to run to the store, and I imagine the Lord in the car with me. I say, "Okay Lord, what should we get today? Chicken, sausage, or steak? Lord, do these pants make me look fat?"

Does that sound ridiculous? Well, I am practicing His presence. Wherever you go and whatever you do, take Him with you... even to the bathroom. (Hey, it is nothing the Lord has not already seen before.)

Maybe you are watching the kids, going for a walk, or answering phones in the office. It does not matter. You do not have to talk to Him out loud all the time... People might think you are a little crazy (especially at work), but you can imagine Him there with you at all times.

It is actually not so far from reality because He is there. He is inside of you. The key is to bring Him to your mind and remember that He is there. When you do that, you cannot get away with doing what you usually do.

It Puts You in a Place to Hear His Voice

Practicing His presence brings conviction and puts you in a place to hear His voice. Since you are imagining Him there all the time, pictures will continually come to your mind. You will feel impressions much stronger than before because He is right there, and He is the one bringing them up.

While you are imagining Him there ask, "Lord, should I go to this meeting?" You will realize that you know the answer already. *No*, that is not something the Lord would do or, *yes*, it is.

When the Lord is with you, it changes all your decisions. You are tuning into your spirit all the time. It is like flipping through radio channels and where you mostly heard static before, you will hear a clear voice ring through.

PILLAR POINT:

When you practice His presence and learn to hear that still, small voice in your spirit, it is like finding the right frequency on the radio.

The Love Relationship

When you come to the place of walking in that relationship with the Lord Jesus, the gifts, call, and anointing will fall into line.

Paul gets us all fired up about the gifts of the Spirit in 1 Corinthians 12, only to end on the strangest low note. After ranting about how all of us have a place and how the Holy Spirit manifests the gifts through us, He ends by saying, "...but let me show you a better way."

Chapter 13 is the better way. It is the chapter on love.

As you come into this relationship with Jesus you will finally understand the passage that says:

> *1 Corinthians 13:8 Love never fails. But whether there are prophecies, they will fail; whether there are tongues, they will cease; whether there is knowledge, it will vanish away.*

PILLAR POINT:

That is the point of learning to hear God's voice. The purpose is not to prophesy or *get revelation*. The point of it all is to come into the perfect knowledge of agape love.

It is only in Jesus' presence that you will experience this love. It is only through hearing His voice for yourself that you won't just feel this love but will also be able to pour it out.

RAPID RECAP

1. *God is always speaking to you in the still, small voice.*
2. *The voice will come out of your own spirit and will sound like you but won't say it as you would.*
3. *The voice will be gentle and not pushy.*
4. *Practicing the Lord's presence positions you to hear His voice all the time.*

11

#8 HEARING GOD THROUGH CIRCUMSTANCES

You have learned how to hear God through the Word and the Spirit. As a result, your cement is well mixed, and you love flowing in the Spirit and hearing from the Word.

The question remains though: How do you know if your ideas are from the Lord? Well, that is what you need this chapter for. The Lord will *seal* the revelation He gave you by confirming it through others.

It all starts out when you feel an impression in your spirit that you are called to something specific. The Word also confirms what you think.

Then, one day you are in a meeting and the preacher shares what has been on your heart the whole time. When this happens, the Lord is saying, "Lightbulb moment!"

The next thing you know, your circumstances change, and an opportunity opens up. You think, "I wonder if this is God's will for my life?"

Of course, *this* is God's will for your life! He has been confirming His word all along the way. The shift in circumstances is just another confirmation of what He has been telling you all along.

If there is a shift in your circumstances but you are not getting any revelation and the Lord has not been speaking to you in any of the other seven ways, I caution you to wait a while.

The Lord will follow a very specific protocol when speaking to you through circumstances.

Word, Spirit, Circumstances – The Full Package

If the doors are not opening for your plan, maybe you are basing your revelation on the wrong signs because God always confirms His word to us.

He speaks through the Word first; He will confirm that message through the Spirit, and only then will He make it clear through your circumstances.

God does not reveal His will to you through *either* the Word, the Spirit, or circumstances. Rather, He confirms His will through all three!

That is how you know it is God's will. Isn't that incredible? You do not need to go around looking for signs.

When you already have the impression in your spirit, the signs will follow.

Say for example, you have been seeking the Lord to start a new ministry venture. You have a fire in your heart that indicates that you need to get moving forward in your ministry. You feel this is really of the Lord.

Then you get into the Scriptures and read about when the Lord said to Moses, "Go and set my people free."

You think, "That burns in me. There is something in that word!" Suddenly the Lord opens an opportunity for you to get involved in a ministry.

Then, you wonder if it is of God...? Of course, it is of God! He has been talking to you and leading you up to this point. I am not saying you won't face warfare getting to this point, but that is another book altogether.

God Uses Circumstances to Confirm

The point is, God uses circumstances to confirm the message that He has already given to you.

There is, however, a big caution in just using circumstances as a sign. The world does that all the time.

"Two birds flew over me. It is a sign that I must go in two directions at once."

"I saw two turtle doves and so the Lord is telling me there is something symbolic about the number two. He is saying my ministry has a double purpose."

Definitely not! The signs that God uses in circumstances should confirm what you have already received from the Word and from the Spirit.

PILLAR POINT:

Circumstances follow the message from God to confirm, not the other way around.

You shouldn't be asking, "Lord, what are you telling me here?" God should have already told you, if you were listening. The circumstance is just a confirmation.

I get this all the time. I will be journaling, and the Lord will say, "You need to concentrate more on this particular kind of counseling. You are weak in this area and I want you to study." I read the Word and suddenly everywhere in the Scriptures, I see the Lord bringing up the same point.

Next thing you know, we get phone calls and knocks on the door with people who have these exact counseling needs. To me, this is just a confirmation of what God has been saying all along.

I will ask the Lord when He wants us to host a seminar. Then, I will feel in my spirit that it is time, and I will say to my husband, "I feel we need to talk on this topic at the next seminar."

Then, as I am in the Word, the revelation starts to flow about what we will preach. Someone on my team will contact me and ask, "Mom, are we having a seminar any time soon because people keep calling in and asking when the next seminar will be"?

Bring the Pictures Together

That is how I hear the voice of God. You just need to bring all the pictures together. Instead, you are waiting for this big voice to come out of the sky.

Confirmation Through Other People

In addition to confirming His will for you through circumstances, the Lord will also speak to you through people.

You might be having a conversation, and someone says something that either really annoys you, or really encourages you... but it just somehow has an impact you cannot shake. Somehow it hits you, and you realize, "That was God's voice!"

You may not always like it and it may not always be pretty, but you can neither go left nor right because you know that was God. If you have been pushing down the Word and sensing things in your spirit, you will recognize it.

You will go to a church meeting and it will seem that the preacher is speaking directly to you.

"Oh well, that was just the preacher."

No, that was the voice of God. He might have been using another man to speak, but you just heard the will of God for your life. What are you doing with it?

God uses so many different ways to get our attention. You just need to wake up and listen to it. Sometimes I am going through, and I am triggering all over the place.

Then my youngest daughter, Ruby, would say something out of her childlike innocence and it would feel like a sword went right through my heart. That was God's voice. I better listen to it! That was not a child speaking but God.

Learn to identify that in others. Like I said, you may not always like it.

Identify His Voice

By now you should be able to sense when there is something powerful contained in the words others are speaking. They said of Jesus, "Never a man spoke as this man." Why? It was because of the power with which He spoke.

They could see the same power manifest in the disciples when they spoke. God will use people around you. He will use children. He will use preachers. He will use prophets. He will use whoever is available for Him to use!

Sometimes someone will be talking, and you will think, "That is a bunch of bubble and froth!" At other times, people will speak, and you will note, "Oh yes, that is God. I feel that. There is something about what they just said that impacted my life."

Confirmation Through Teaching

The Lord can also lead you to books or websites, which is how many find us.

You might find yourself on a website reading an article that feels as if you are not just reading something the author wrote, but something the Lord is saying to you directly. It strikes your heart. You just heard God's voice and His will for your life.

Turn up the Volume

Let's put it all together. You have been hearing the will of God for your life all along. You just have not identified it. What you can do now is take the principles I have taught you and turn the volume up on the radio.

This way, His word becomes a little clearer and you do not have to spend hours and hours in the Word before you start receiving impressions in your spirit.

The wonderful thing about your spiritual walk is that it is a progression. It won't happen in one day. If you are not there yet, it does not matter. There is a goal, and you can go as far as you need or want to go.

Start where you are in this moment. Put pictures in your heart using the Word. Learn to listen to the impressions of your spirit during the day. Always practice His presence and keep Him close by.

Then, also be on the lookout for the articles you stumble across, the Christians you bump into, or the preacher you are listening to. As you take the cement, water, and bricks, everything will be put together and you will have a sturdy house built on a solid foundation.

RAPID RECAP

1. *God will speak through your circumstance as a confirmation of what He has already told you.*
2. *The Lord will use others to speak to you on His behalf.*
3. *Learning to hear Him in many ways increases your ability to hear Him in anyone He chooses to use in your life.*

12

THE ULTIMATE PURPOSE
FOR HEARING HIS VOICE

Have you noticed how easily people rub off on you? You make a new friend and before you know it, you are using phrases they use. It is quite the thing in our ministry.

Because we are such an international ministry with team members from all over the world, we have rubbed off on each other to the point that you can hear a whole variety of phrases around the dinner table.

Someone will ask for the salt in German, another will answer in Spanish while someone throws a typical American slang.

You will notice that each church and community have a language of their own. Your mindsets and likes will be influenced by those around you. It is the way the Lord created us. He created us to connect with those around us.

Well, imagine for a moment that the Lord was the one doing most of the rubbing off on you...

How is this going to happen?

PILLAR POINT:

The only way it can take place is when you put yourself in a position to hear His voice often. Soon you will use His catch phrases.

You will find His agape love rubbing off on you. Soon your walk with Him won't be about *gifts* and revelations but completely about relationship.

When you get to that point, then you have something to hand out to the body of Christ.

Experience Him in All Five Senses!

So, do not limit yourself! I have taught on different ways to hear His voice, but what I have really done is to teach you how to hear, see, feel, smell, and taste His voice.

I have taught you to be sensitive to the messages that are coming from your spirit. Now, imagine that you can combine them all.

Give it a try next time you are in His presence. Try to involve all your senses in hearing Him.

When you come to the Lord to receive direction, whether that is through prayer or journaling, be mindful of the following things:

1. What visions am I seeing? What pictures are coming up in my mind?
2. What sounds am I hearing? Am I hearing words or a specific sound?
3. What do I feel inside of me? Urim? Thummim? Warning? Joy?
4. What do I smell in the spirit? Am I aware of a fragrance?
5. What do I taste in the spirit? Is there something sweet in the air?

Give it a try! By doing that, you allow yourself to experience the Lord in His fullness. It means that you are completely engaged with Him. It won't take long at all and the nature of the Lord will begin to show in you.

You see, that is what the fruit of the Spirit is all about.

PILLAR POINT:

Have you ever wondered how to develop the fruit of the Spirit in your life? Well, this is the secret: Experience Jesus!

The more you are wrapped up in Him, the quicker you pick up His nature and along with that every fruit of the Spirit. This is the natural progression every believer goes through.

However, before you can claim yourself the expert on hearing God it is a good idea to learn each way.

By this stage of your journey, you realize that it is about a lot more than just *hearing His voice*. It is in fact about *becoming the image of Christ*.

With that revelation, you are fast on your way to establishing the church as a city on a hill! Your life is the light that shines in the darkness.

ABOUT THE AUTHOR

B orn in Bulawayo, Zimba-
bwe and raised in South
Africa, Colette had a zeal to
serve the Lord from a young age.
Coming from a long line of Christian leaders and having grown
up as a pastor's kid, she is no
stranger to the realities of ministry. Despite having to endure
many hardships such as her parents' divorce, rejection, and
poverty, she continues to follow
after the Lord passionately.
Overcoming these obstacles early in her life has built a foundation of compassion and desire to help others gain victory
in their lives.

Since then, the Lord led Colette, with her husband, Craig
Toach, to establish *Apostolic Movement International* and
Toach Ministries International.

Apostolic Movement International focuses on training those
called to the fivefold ministry whereas *Toach Ministries International* ministers to, covers, supports, and spiritually parents like-minded leaders.

In addition, Colette is a fantastic cook, an amazing mom to
not only her four natural children, but to her numerous spiritual children all over the world. Colette is also a renowned
author, mentor, trainer, and a woman that has great taste in
shoes! The scripture to "be all things to all men" definitely

applies to her, and the Lord keeps adding to that list of things each and every day.

How does she do it all? Experience through every book and teaching the life of an apostle firsthand and get the insight into how the call of God can make every aspect of your life an incredible adventure.

Read more at www.colettetoach.com

Connect with Colette Toach on Facebook!
www.facebook.com/ColetteToach

Check Colette out on Amazon.com at:
www.amazon.com/author/colettetoach

OTHER BOOKS BY COLETTE TOACH

If you enjoyed this book, I know you will also love the following books.

Persistent Prayer

Angels and Demons at Work

ISBN: 978-1-62664-220-1

Prayer is our connection to the Lord. It takes the will of God in heaven and brings it down to the earth. It removes the hindrances that stand in the way, allows man to hear God, and blocks the enemy completely! When you couple this with someone who is ready to speak, obey, and do the will of God in this earth, you get a recipe for a highly successful prayer life.

Colette's full book collection on...

Kindle and...   iBooks.

The Way of Dreams and Visions

Your Secret Conversation with God

ISBN: 978-1-62664-002-3

God Everybody has dreams - it is a well-known fact. But what not everyone knows is that the Lord is talking to you right now through your dreams.

Now you don't have to be a prophet to receive dreams and visions from the Lord, or to understand them. You can understand what the Lord is telling you, right now.

The Way of Dreams and Visions Symbol Dictionary 2017 Edition

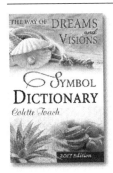

ISBN: 978-1-62664-149-5

Trying to interpret your dreams is sometimes a lot like traveling to another country for the first time. Having no road map to point out landmarks or to show you what direction you need to go can cause a lot of confusion.

In this dictionary, Apostle Colette Toach is going to do more then just explain simple symbols to you - she is going to help you decode the messages the Lord is giving you right now.

Online Prophetic School:

www.prophetic-school.com

Hands on mentorship, training and teaching for the Next Gen Prophet! Sign up for your one-on-one interview today!

Next Gen Prophets Podcast at Charisma Podcast Network:

Join Colette and Craig on their podcast called Next Gen Prophets at Charisma Podcast Network:

REACH OUT!

Connect with Craig and Colette Toach Personally:
www.toach-ministries.com

Facebook: www.facebook.com/toachministries

YouTube: https://www.youtube.com/toachministries

Get Colette's books at AMI Bookshop:
www.ami-bookshop.com

Get Colette's books on Amazon.com:
www.amazon.com/author/colettetoach

Do you have any questions about any products?

Contact us at: +1 (760) 466 - 7257

(9am to 5pm California Time, Tuesday – Saturday)

E-mail Address: ctoach@toach-ministries.com

Postal Address:

> Craig and Colette Toach
> 5663 Balboa Ave #416
> San Diego, CA 92111, USA

NOTES

Chapter 4: #2 Hearing God Through the Urim and Thummim

[1] Toach, Colette. *Prophetic Function*. Prophetic Field Guide Series, Vol. 2. 2nd ed. San Diego, California: Apostolic Movement International LLC, 2016

Chapter 5: #3 Hearing God Through Dreams

[2] Toach, Colette. *The Way of Dreams and Visions: Interpreting Your Secret Conversion with God*. 3rd ed. San Diego, California: Apostolic Movement International LLC, 2016

[3] Toach, Colette. *The Way of Dreams and Visions Symbol Dictionary 2017 Edition*. 3rd ed. San Diego, California: Apostolic Movement International LLC, 2016

Chapter 6: #4 Hearing God Through Visions

[5] Toach, Colette. *The Way of Dreams and Visions Symbol Dictionary 2017 Edition*. 3rd ed. San Diego, California: Apostolic Movement International LLC, 2016

[6] Toach, Colette. *The Way of Dreams and Visions: Interpreting Your Secret Conversion with God*. 3rd ed. San Diego, California: Apostolic Movement International LLC, 2016

Chapter 7: #5 Hearing God Through Tongues and Utterance

[7] Toach, Colette. *Prophetic Function*. Prophetic Field Guide Series, Vol. 2. 2nd ed. San Diego, California: Apostolic Movement International LLC, 2016

Chapter 8: #6 Hearing God Through Journaling

[8] Toach, Colette. *The Way of Dreams and Visions: Interpreting Your Secret Conversion with God*. 3rd ed. San Diego, California: Apostolic Movement International LLC, 2016

[9] Toach, Colette. *Practical Prophetic Ministry: The Metamorphosis of the Prophet*. 3rd ed. San Diego, California: Apostolic Movement International LLC, 2016

[10] Toach, Colette. *Called to the Ministry: Helping You Find the Place Where You Belong.* 2nd ed. San Diego, California: Apostolic Movement International LLC, 2016

Made in the USA
Columbia, SC
08 March 2025

54886842R00070